ESSENTIAL FISH & GAME COOKBOOK

Delicious Recipes from Shore Lunches to Gourmet Dinners

Recipe Conversions

Use the following conversion chart for liquids and larger dry ingredient measurements. Since the masses of some dry ingredients (pastes, ground herbs, etc.) will be different depending on how they are manufactured, you should research the correct conversion for the exact ingredient you are using.

⅛ teaspoon = 0.6 mL	½ cup = 120 mL
¼ teaspoon = 1.2 mL	¾ cup = 175 mL
½ teaspoon = 2.5 mL	1 cup = 240 mL
1 teaspoon = 5 mL	1 fluid ounce = 30 mL
½ tablespoon = 7.5 mL	1 ounce = 28 grams
1 tablespoon = 15 mL	1 fluid pound = 500 mL
⅛ cup = 30 mL	1 pound = 453 grams
¼ cup = 60 mL	

ISBN 978-1-4971-0491-4

Library of Congress Control Number: 2024915654

To learn more about the other great books from Fox Chapel Publishing, or to find a retailer near you, call toll-free 800-457-9112, send mail to: 903 Square Street, Mount Joy, PA 17552, or visit us at *www.FoxChapelPublishing.com*.

We are always looking for talented authors. To submit an idea, please send a brief inquiry to acquisitions@foxchapelpublishing.com.

Printed in China
First printing

ESSENTIAL

FISH

&

GAME

COOKBOOK

Delicious Recipes from Shore Lunches to Gourmet

Edited by Scott Leysath, The Sporting Chef

FOX CHAPEL
PUBLISHING

Salmon is a versatile and nutritious fish—effortlessly enhanced with just a few simple flavors to create delicious, satisfying meals.

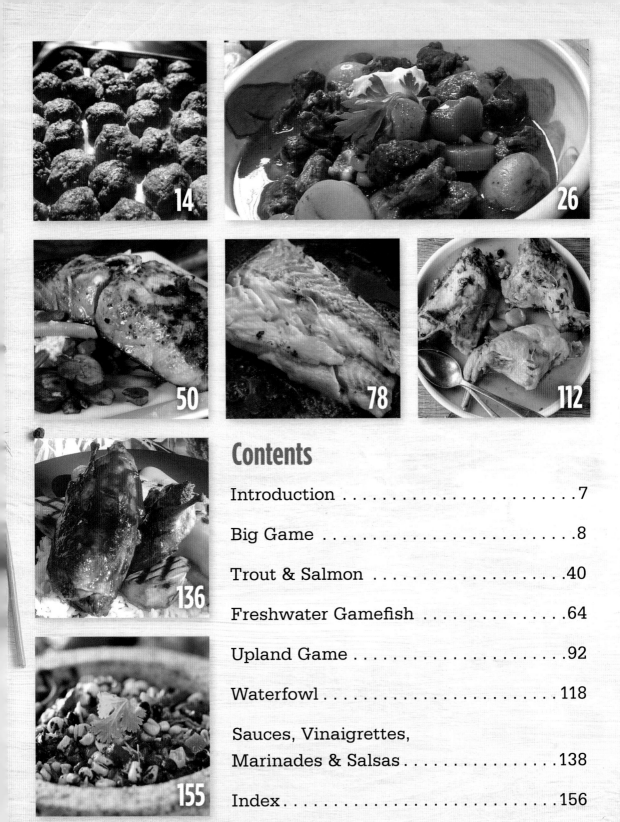

14

26

50

78

112

136

155

Contents

Your perfectly prepared
fresh catch makes for
the most satisfying of
shore lunches.

Introduction

Whether you crave the outdoor experience or simply want to hone your skills as a fish-and-game cook, this cookbook is loaded with recipes that will help make your harvest taste better than ever. Over the past few decades, home cooks have discovered that wild fish and game, from beautiful elk loin to farm pond bluegill, makes for exceptional table fare.

The recipes in this book are all intended to provide the people who hunt and fish (and the lucky friends and neighbors who also profit from their harvest) with the best possible information and tools to create meals that go beyond just tasting good. These techniques, dishes, and serving suggestions have benefited from the expert eye of Scott Leysath, the longtime host of the popular Outdoor Channel show *The Sporting Chef.* Whether you're slowly braising your elk roast at home with a side of roasted vegetables or battering your catch lakeside for a classic shore lunch, these expert-level, innovative menus for everything from Grilled Elk Chops to Quail and Goat Cheese Stuffed Chiles will add variety and flavor to your culinary adventures.

Big Game

Venison is the protein of choice for hunters across much of North America. But what do you do with the meat after the harvest? The answer: the options are almost limitless, as the recipes in this chapter show.

In the United States, deer are the most popularly hunted species of game with around 6 million harvested each year. By comparison, the elk harvest is typically less than 200,000 animals. Compared with most other countries, the opportunity is there for American hunters to bring home a freezer full of deer venison each season. But then what?

In the Field, Get the Meat in the Cooler Quickly

Field care is a critical component of wild game excellence. Once on the ground, get your animals gutted immediately and cooled as soon as possible. Driving around with your deer in the back of your pickup on a warm fall day to show your neighbors you were successful can allow bacteria to compromise the meat. Ice is important: make sure to bring along enough to cool your game for the drive home.

Aging antlered game will make the difference between meat that is tough or tender. Properly aged meat that has been hung in a 34°F to 39°F cooler for a week or two will be more tender and taste less gamey than meat butchered immediately. If you have unaged roasts in the freezer, their flavor and tenderness can be improved by placing them on a rack (with a pan underneath to catch any drippings), uncovered, for five to seven days.

As with anything edible, do not take chances with questionable game meats. If it smells bad, there is a reason why. Do not try and mask the aroma of bad meat with potent marinades. There is a reason why it looks or smells bad. Take the hint and discard it.

The Ins and Outs of Preparing Venison

How you cook your deer depends on the age, sex, and which part of the animal is going on the grill. The most tender muscles—loins, tenderloins, and trimmed hindquarters—are best cooked fast and hot. Fire up the grill or skillet and sear the meat on all sides until the desired internal temperature is reached. Deer meat has virtually no fat, and cooking beyond medium-rare, or about 135°F, will result in a piece of meat that is tough and somewhat off-tasting, or gamey. But if you like it well-done, that's entirely your choice.

Tougher cuts like shanks, neck roasts, and shoulders should be cooked slowly to break down the sinew that occurs in muscles that are used most often. Loins and tenderloins just go along for the ride. Shanks and shoulders do much of the work moving animals around the woods while avoiding predators. A medium-rare shoulder steak is going to be much tougher than one cut from the loin or hindquarter. Save the better cuts for the grill and the tough ones for the slow cooker.

Unlike beef fat, big game fat is rarely good to eat. Venison should be trimmed of as much visible fat as possible before cooking and many cooks add fats like bacon and butter to flavor their game. (Who would argue that a venison backstrap wrapped in bacon doesn't taste better than one without bacon?)

The main difference between wild and farmed meats is the fat content. A fatty beef ribeye from the grocery store, for example, is forgiving when the cook happens to overcook it. It might not be as red in the center as desired, but fat is flavor. Lean game meats, on the other hand, generally require less cooking time than farmed meats and, if overcooked, they will be tough and "gamey"— the dreaded word used to imply that something is off-tasting. Not to fear: this book shows you how to cook game meats perfectly.

The combination of salt and pepper is a basic yet effective seasoning for a perfectly grilled venison steak.

Grilled Venison Steaks

A venison steak grilled to perfection and seasoned only with salt and pepper is an amazing feat and will delight the palate. However, if you'd like yours a little on the spicy side, this one is for you. Jalapeños give it that slight kick of spice. Once you've mastered this dish, you will have officially proven yourself as both a big game hunter and camp cook.

Ingredients

- » 2 jalapeños
- » 1 cup butter
- » ¼ cup lemon juice, plus more to taste (optional)
- » 2 teaspoons salt
- » 1 teaspoon pepper
- » 2 tablespoons Worcestershire sauce, plus more to taste (optional)
- » Four 12-ounce venison tenderloin or round steaks

Makes: 2 to 4 servings

Prep Time: 10 minutes, plus 2 hours marinating

Cook Time: 8 to 14 minutes

Preparation

1. Cut the jalapeños into slices, removing any seeds. In a medium saucepan over medium-high heat, place the butter, lemon juice, salt, pepper, Worcestershire sauce, and jalapeño slices. Bring the mixture to a boil. Remove the marinade from heat and let it cool slightly.

2. Place the venison steaks in a square glass baking dish. Pour the marinade over the steaks. Cover the baking dish and place it in the refrigerator for 30 minutes to 2 hours to marinate. The longer the steaks marinate, the stronger the flavor will be.

3. Preheat the grill. Remove the steaks from the refrigerator and discard the marinade. Grill the steaks over low heat or coals for approximately 4 to 7 minutes on each side, turning once, until the steaks are hot and grilled to your desired doneness. If desired, baste the steaks with additional lemon juice or Worcestershire sauce during or after grilling.

Horseradish Venison Burgers

These spirited burgers combine lean venison, spicy horseradish, and bacon—a combination made in heaven. Like any burgers, these can be made broiled, grilled, or pan-seared, depending on time of year and the occasion. Serve on your preferred buns and with your favorite cheese (if you're making cheeseburgers) and fixings and let your guests help themselves.

Makes: 4 servings
Prep Time: 10 minutes
Cook Time: 10 to 12 minutes

These burgers are versatile since you can make them broiled, grilled, or pan-seared.

Ingredients

» 1 pound ground venison
» ½ cup seasoned breadcrumbs
» ¼ cup minced onion
» 1 to 2 tablespoons prepared horseradish
» 1 tablespoon ketchup
» 1 teaspoon salt
» ½ teaspoon black pepper
» ½ teaspoon ground sage
» Dash Worcestershire sauce
» 4 slices bacon

Preparation

1. In a large mixing bowl, mix the venison by hand with the breadcrumbs, minced onion, horseradish, ketchup, salt, pepper, sage, and Worcestershire sauce. Shape the mixture into 4 patties.

2. Wrap a piece of bacon around each patty and secure it with a toothpick or skewer.

3. Broil, grill, or pan-sear each side until done. If using, melt a slice of cheese over the top of each patty.

Venison Meatloaf with a Kick

What might be just a kick to some isn't spicy at all to others: experiment with different spices, chile peppers, and sauces to reach a heat level to your liking. You can also add your own personal touch to the texture of the meatloaf with roasted peppers, grilled corn kernels, or red pepper flakes or any combination of those. And as long as you're making meatloaf, you might as well make an extra one to freeze for later—it's super easy to make.

Ingredients

- » 1 tablespoon vegetable oil
- » 1 cup diced onion
- » 1 cup diced celery
- » ½ cup diced bell pepper
- » 3 garlic cloves, minced
- » 8 saltine crackers
- » 1 egg
- » ¾ pound ground venison
- » ¼ pound ground pork
- » 2 tablespoons brown sugar
- » ½ teaspoons spicy brown mustard
- » ¼ cup minced cilantro leaves
- » ¼ teaspoon ground thyme
- » Dash paprika
- » 3 tablespoons ketchup
- » 1 tablespoon brown sugar

Makes: 4 servings

Prep Time:
15 minutes

Cook Time:
50 minutes

Preparation

1. Preheat the oven to 350°F. Heat the vegetable oil in a medium skillet over medium heat. Add the onion, celery, and bell pepper to the pan and cook until the onions are translucent. Add the garlic and cook for 1 minute. Remove the pan from heat and allow the mixture to cool.

2. Crush the saltine crackers and lightly beat the egg. In a large bowl, combine the crackers, egg, venison, pork, and half the brown sugar and mix by hand until well combined. Add the mustard, cilantro, thyme, and paprika. Mix again until all the ingredients are well combined and evenly incorporated. Add the cooled onion mixture and mix well.

3. Lightly pat the mixture into a 5 x 9–inch loaf pan or 9-inch-square baking dish. Bake uncovered for 40 minutes or until the internal temperature of the meatloaf registers 160°F on a meat thermometer.

4. Meanwhile, in a medium bowl, combine the ketchup and remaining 1 tablespoon of brown sugar and mix well. Spread the ketchup mixture evenly over the top of the cooked meatloaf. Return the loaf to the oven for an additional 10 minutes.

5. To serve, remove the loaf from the oven and let it cool in the pan for 5 minutes before cutting it into slices or squares.

Adding your preferred spices will give this meatloaf as much of a kick as you need.

Many starches and sides go well with this savory dish.

Barbecued Venison Meatballs

Go with mashed potatoes, rice, or noodles as the base for a full meal using these meatballs or keep them in the slow cooker with toothpicks at hand for a fine party appetizer. If you want to make a double or triple batch and freeze them for later, it's easy: place the cooked meatballs on a lightly greased pan and freeze them completely before vacuum-sealing or placing them in freezer-safe bags.

Makes: About 20 meatballs

Prep Time: 10 minutes, plus 2 hours marinating

Cook Time: 1 hour and 15 minutes

Ingredients

- » 1 egg
- » 1 pound ground venison
- » ½ pound ground pork
- » ½ cup dry breadcrumbs
- » 1 teaspoon salt, plus ¼ teaspoon
- » Pepper, to taste
- » 1 cup ketchup
- » 1 tablespoon Worcestershire sauce
- » 2 tablespoons brown sugar
- » 2 tablespoons vinegar

Preparation

1. Using a fork, lightly whisk the egg in the bottom of a large bowl. Add the venison, pork, breadcrumbs, salt, and pepper. Mix by hand until well combined. Shape the mixture into 1-inch meatballs and place the meatballs in a 9 x 13–inch glass baking dish.

2. In a medium bowl, combine the ketchup, Worcestershire sauce, brown sugar, vinegar, ¼ teaspoon salt, and pepper. Pour the sauce over the meatballs in the baking dish. Cover the baking dish with aluminum foil and place the meatballs and sauce in the refrigerator for 2 to 24 hours.

3. Preheat the oven to 350°F. Place the covered meatballs dish in the oven and bake for 1 hour and 15 minutes, basting once or twice with the sauce from the bottom of the dish. To serve, spoon the meatballs and sauce onto serving plates.

Breaded Venison Steaks in Wine Sauce

If you are a successful deer hunter, there is a good chance that your freezer has a fair amount of cubed or round steaks that have been tenderized. This recipe is a perfect way to cook and serve them. Invite friends and family over and show them how good venison steaks can really be.

Makes: 4 to 8 servings

Prep Time: 15 minutes

Cook Time: 1½ hours

You can use this recipe to clear out your stored meats.

Ingredients

» 1 egg
» 1 sleeve of round butter crackers
» ½ cup flour
» Salt and pepper, to taste
» Four to eight 12-ounce venison round or cubed steaks
» 4 tablespoons vegetable oil
» 1 onion
» 2 cups mushrooms, sliced
» 1 cup red wine

Preparation

1. Preheat the oven to 350°F. In a small shallow bowl, beat the egg. Crush the crackers into fine crumbs and place them in a separate, shallow dish. Add the flour, salt, and pepper to the crushed crackers and mix well. Dip each venison steak first into the egg and then into the cracker mixture, turning to coat both sides.

2. In a large skillet over medium-high heat, heat the vegetable oil. Add the coated steaks to the hot oil, turning quickly to brown both sides. Only the outsides of the steaks should be browned. Transfer the steaks to a baking dish.

3. Chop the onion and drain the mushrooms. Place the onions and mushrooms over the steaks in the baking dish. Pour the red wine over the top. Cover the baking dish with aluminum foil and bake for 1½ hours.

4. To serve, place one steak on each plate and spoon some of the sauce, mushrooms, and onions from the baking dish over each serving.

Broiled Venison Patties

These versatile patties can be used for burgers, sliders, or broken up and added to spaghetti sauce for a bolognese. But start with the burgers, because who wouldn't love a homemade venison burger? Set out a variety of fixings so your guests can load them up in the ways they like best.

Makes: 12 small patties or 6 large patties
Prep Time: 10 to 15 minutes
Cook Time: 5 to 10 minutes

Ingredients

- 2 tablespoons butter
- ½ small onion
- 2 tablespoons chopped celery
- 1 teaspoon dried parsley flakes
- ¾ pound ground venison
- ½ cup crackers, finely crushed
- ¼ cup milk
- 1 egg
- 1 tablespoon flour
- 2 teaspoons lemon juice
- Dash garlic powder
- Dash pepper

Preparation

1. In a small saucepan over medium-high heat, melt the butter. Chop the onion. Add the onion, celery, and parsley flakes to the saucepan and sauté until the onion is tender. Transfer the sautéed onion mixture to a medium bowl.

2. To the bowl, add the venison, crackers, milk, egg, flour, lemon juice, garlic powder, and pepper and mix by hand until well combined.

3. Shape the mixture into patties. Fry the patties in a skillet over medium-high heat until browned; or place the patties under an oven broiler for 2 to 3 minutes on each side.

Venison patties make for deeply flavorful burgers!

Herbed Venison Roast with Cranberry Chutney

Cooking a proper venison roast takes a little practice. If you prefer the meat cooked beyond medium, you might consider a low-and-slow preparation that results in something more like pot roast. Paired with a fine red wine, this dish makes for a great special-occasion dinner.

Makes: 4 servings per pound of roast
Prep Time: 25 minutes
Cook Time: 15 minutes per pound

Ingredients

Cranberry Chutney

» 1 cup diced onion
» 1 cup brown sugar, plus more as needed
» 1 cup dried cranberries
» ¾ cup cranberry juice
» ⅓ cup freshly squeezed lemon juice, plus more as needed
» 2 garlic cloves, minced
» 2 tablespoons minced fresh rosemary leaves
» Pinch salt, plus more to taste
» Pinch pepper, plus more to taste

Roast

» One 2- to 4-pound venison shoulder roast
» 1 to 2 tablespoons dried Provençal herbs
» Salt and pepper, to taste
» ½ to 1 pound bacon

Preparation

1. Preheat the oven to 500°F. **Prepare the Cranberry Chutney.** Place all the ingredients in a saucepan over medium heat. Bring the mixture to a boil, then lower the heat to low and simmer until the mixture is reduced by about one-third and has thickened. Stir in the lemon juice. Season to taste with additional salt and pepper. Too sweet? Add more lemon juice. Too sour? Add more brown sugar. Puree the chutney in a blender.

2. Rub all sides of the roast with the Provençal herbs and season liberally with salt and pepper. Wrap the roast with overlapping bacon strips and tie with kitchen string or drape the strips of bacon over the roast. Place the roast on a rack in a shallow roasting pan.

3. Brush the pureed chutney over the bacon-wrapped roast. Place the roasting pan in the preheated oven and reduce the temperature to 400°F. Roast uncovered for 15 minutes per pound. For medium-rare, the internal temperature should be 130 to 135 degrees.

4. To serve, slice the roast across the grain. Transfer the slices to serving plates and garnish with the Cranberry Chutney.

A glass of red wine pairs well with this dish.

Oven-Baked Venison Sausage

If you have never tried making sausage, this recipe is a great place to start, especially if you have venison ready at hand. It requires no special equipment. If you take to the task, graduate from this recipe to using this recipe as a template, adding special ingredients to create your own signature game sausage.

Makes: about 10 servings

Prep Time: 15 minutes, plus 24 hours chilling

Cook Time: 1 hour and 20 minutes

Ingredients

- » 2 pounds ground venison
- » 2 tablespoons liquid smoke flavoring
- » ¼ teaspoon garlic powder
- » 1 teaspoon mustard seed
- » ⅛ teaspoon pepper
- » ½ teaspoon onion salt
- » 1 cup water
- » 2 tablespoons tenderizing salt

Preparation

1. In a large bowl, combine all the ingredients and mix by hand until well combined.

2. Place a 12 x 18–inch length of aluminum foil on a flat surface, shiny side up. Shape the venison mixture into a log of desired thickness. Place the log on the foil and wrap it tightly in the foil, securing the ends. Place the wrapped log in the refrigerator for at least 24 hours.

3. Preheat the oven to 325°F. Pierce holes in the bottom of the aluminum foil and set the wrapped log on a jellyroll pan or baking sheet with an edge. Bake for 1 hour and 20 minutes. Carefully remove the wrapped log and let it cool for 10 minutes before placing it in the refrigerator to chill for at least 24 hours before slicing.

4. To serve, slice the sausage, cutting through the aluminum foil. Peel the aluminum foil off each slice before serving.

The secret to a great baked sausage is giving it time to cool and form for one day before serving.

Venison Tips with Seasoned Rice & Peppers

This is a perfect recipe for cuts from the hindquarter. With the vegetables, tenderized venison, and rice all in one dish, it's a complete meal.

Makes: 4 servings
Prep Time: 10 to 15 minutes
Cook Time: 20 minutes

Ingredients

» 1 cup long-grain rice
» ½ cup broken vermicelli pasta
» ¼ cup minced fresh Italian parsley
» 1 teaspoon onion powder
» ¼ teaspoon garlic powder
» ⅛ teaspoon dried thyme
» 2 tablespoons butter
» 2½ cups beef broth
» 1 small onion
» 1 green bell pepper
» 1 red bell pepper
» 1 tablespoon vegetable oil
» 1 pound venison, trimmed of any fat or gristle and cut into 1- to 2-inch cubes

Preparation

1. In a medium bowl, combine the rice, vermicelli, parsley, onion powder, garlic powder, and thyme and mix until evenly incorporated.

2. In a large heavy saucepan over medium-high heat, combine the butter and the beef broth. Cover the saucepan and bring to a boil. Meanwhile, chop the onion and cut the peppers into thin strips.

3. Add the rice mixture, onion, and peppers to the boiling broth. Cover the saucepan and reduce the heat to medium-low. Allow the rice to simmer for 15 minutes or until the rice is tender.

4. Heat the vegetable oil in a large skillet over medium-high heat. Add the venison to the skillet; cook and stir until the venison is nicely browned on the outside and almost cooked through.

5. Add the browned venison to the rice while it is still simmering. Continue to simmer until the venison and peppers are tender. Toss the rice, venison, and peppers together with a fork. To serve, divide the rice mixture onto plates and top with the meat and vegetables.

Fresh bell peppers cooked just right add that bit of crunch!

This dish can be made in a skillet but is also great on the grill.

Venison Bulgogi

The marinated Korean-style venison flank is also great cooked on a hot grill. Korean for "fire" (bul) "meat" (gogi), bulgogi makes thinly sliced and marinated strips of meat into an umami-rich, delicious dining experience, and it's a great way to expand your venison-cooking skills.

Makes: 3 to 4 servings

Prep Time: 15 minutes, plus 6 hours marinating

Cook Time: 6 to 10 minutes

Ingredients

- » 1 pound venison flank steak, firmly packed
- » ⅓ cup soy sauce
- » 2½ tablespoons brown sugar
- » ⅓ cup roughly chopped green onion
- » 1 tablespoon peeled and minced fresh ginger
- » 2 garlic cloves, minced
- » 2 tablespoons toasted sesame seeds
- » 2 tablespoons toasted sesame oil
- » ½ teaspoon freshly ground black pepper
- » 2 tablespoons vegetable or olive oil
- » 2 cups sliced mushrooms
- » 2 cups chopped kale
- » Rice, steamed, as needed, to serve

Preparation

1. Lightly pound the venison flank steaks with a mallet or heavy skillet. In a medium bowl, combine the soy sauce with the brown sugar, green onion, ginger, cloves, sesame seeds, sesame oil, and pepper. Add the venison and toss to coat evenly. Cover the bowl and refrigerate for 6 hours or more.

2. Remove the venison flank from the marinade and reserve the marinade. Heat the vegetable oil in a large skillet over high heat. Cook the meat for 2 to 3 minutes on one side, then flip it over and cook for 1 minute. Remove the flanks from the skillet.

3. Add the mushrooms and cook for 3 to 4 minutes. Add the reserved marinade and bring it to a boil. Add the kale and cook for 1 minute. Slice the flank steaks across the grain into 1- to 2-inch-thick slices. Return them to the pan.

4. To serve, mound warm rice on plates or in bowls and spoon the bulgogi over the rice.

Deer Camp Venison Chili

Think about how great a steaming bowl of deer camp chili sounds after a long day in the woods. Whether yours is in deer camp or in the comfort of your home, this recipe requires very little preparation and a big appetite. It's a late fall or winter classic.

Recipes with little prep are great for a meal at the campsite.

Makes: 10 to 12 servings

Prep Time: 10 to 15 minutes

Cook Time: 25 minutes to 1 hour

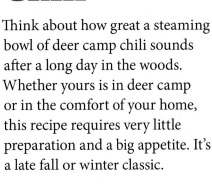

Ingredients

» 1 large onion
» 6 celery stalks
» 2 bell peppers
» 4 jalapeños
» 2 tablespoons vegetable oil
» 2 pounds ground venison
» 1 tablespoon crushed red pepper flakes
» Four 14½-ounce cans Italian-style stewed tomatoes
» One 6-ounce can tomato paste
» One 40-ounce can pinto beans, drained
» 1 teaspoon salt
» 1 teaspoon ground cumin
» 1 to 2 tablespoons chili powder
» White pepper, to taste
» 1 tablespoon sugar
» Sour cream, to serve (optional)
» Corn chips, to serve (optional)
» Green onions, sliced, to serve (optional)

Preparation

1. Chop the onion, celery, and bell peppers. Slice the jalapeños and carefully remove and discard the seeds.

2. Heat the vegetable oil in a large, deep pot over medium-high heat. Add the venison and cook, stirring often, until it is evenly browned. Add the onion, celery, peppers, jalapeños, and red pepper flakes and continue to sauté until the onions are transparent, about 2 to 3 minutes.

3. Add the stewed tomatoes with juice, tomato paste, and pinto beans to the pot and stir well. Continue to cook, stirring often. Add the spices and sugar and reduce the heat to low.

4. Let the chili simmer until ready to serve. To serve, ladle the chili into bowls. If desired, garnish with a dollop of sour cream, a few corn chips, and green onions.

Hunter's Venison Stew

Imagine returning from a challenging day in the woods and being greeted with the wafting aroma of a hearty venison stew. Add a glass of good red wine and some crusty bread and then it's nap time.

Makes: 6 servings
Prep Time: 15 minutes
Cook Time: 30 to 45 minutes

Ingredients

- » 2 pounds venison, cut into 1- to 2-inch cubes
- » 2 tablespoons butter
- » Salt and pepper, to taste
- » 2 cups beef or game broth
- » 2 whole rosemary sprigs
- » 4 garlic cloves, minced
- » 6 carrots
- » 2 large potatoes
- » 3 medium onions
- » 3 celery stalks
- » One 28-ounce can crushed tomatoes

Preparation

1. In a large deep saucepan over medium-high heat, brown the venison in the butter. Season the venison with salt and pepper to taste. Add the broth, rosemary, and garlic. Continue to cook until the venison is tender, about 30 minutes.

2. Meanwhile, peel the carrots and potatoes. Cut the carrots, potatoes, onions, and celery into small pieces. Add the vegetables and crushed tomatoes with juice to the saucepan. Continue to simmer until the potatoes are tender, about 15 minutes.

3. To serve, ladle the soup into bowls.

Venison Cheesesteak

In the tradition of the Philly cheesesteak sandwich, this recipe is a quickie that'll fool some of your friends who claim that they don't like the taste of venison. Get the best rolls and provolone you can find, and you'll wow your friends with the delicious results of your deer harvest.

Makes: 4 servings

Prep Time: 15 minutes

Cook Time: 6 to 10 minutes

Ingredients

» 3 cups venison steak
» Salt and pepper, to taste
» 2 tablespoons olive oil
» 1 large yellow onion, thinly sliced
» 1 green bell pepper, thinly sliced
» 3 garlic cloves
» 2 cups mushrooms, thinly sliced
» Tabasco sauce, to taste
» 8 slices provolone cheese
» 4 Italian rolls, split

Preparation

1. Place the venison in the freezer for 1 hour, or until the meat is almost frozen. Using a sharp, thin-bladed knife, slice the meat as thinly as possible. Allow the meat to thaw completely, wrap it with paper towels to absorb the blood, and season it liberally with salt and pepper.

2. Heat the olive oil in a large, heavy skillet or griddle over medium-high heat. Add the onions, peppers, and garlic and cook until the onions are lightly browned. Add the mushrooms and sauté with the onions and peppers until the onions are soft.

3. Move the vegetables to one side of the skillet and add the sliced venison. Cook the meat until it is lightly browned but not overcooked. Season with a dash or two of Tabasco.

4. Mound the meat into 4 rectangular piles, each about the size of an Italian roll. Top with equal portions of the vegetable mixture. Top each mound with 2 slices of cheese and let the cheese melt.

5. Using two spatulas, scoop up each portion of meat and place them in the rolls.

This filling sandwich is inspired by the classic Philly cheesesteak.

Cubed meat works well in a slow cooker—it will cook through evenly.

Slow Cooker Venison Barbecue

Load up the slow cooker and head to the woods or the water, knowing that a delicious meal awaits your return post-hunt. Slow cookers are especially handy when turning tougher cuts into something tender and delicious.

Makes: 6 servings
Prep Time: 15 minutes
Cook Time: 10 hours

Ingredients

» 1 medium onion
» 4 garlic cloves
» 3 pounds cubed venison
» 1 cup red wine vinegar
» ½ cup Worcestershire sauce
» 2 teaspoons seasoned salt
» 1 pound bacon
» 2 cups ketchup
» ½ cup molasses
» ½ cup brown sugar
» Salt and pepper, to taste
» Rice, potatoes, or toast, to serve

Preparation

1. Dice the onion and mince the garlic. In a 5- or 6-quart slow cooker, place the onion, garlic, venison, red wine vinegar, Worcestershire sauce, tenderizing salt, and seasoned salt. Cover the slow cooker and cook on high for 1 to 2 hours.

2. Meanwhile, in a large skillet over medium-high heat, cook the bacon strips until tender but not crispy. Remove the bacon from the skillet and chop it into ½-inch pieces.

3. Add the cooked bacon, ketchup, molasses, and brown sugar to the slow cooker. Cover the slow cooker and cook on low for 8 to 9 hours. Season to taste with salt and pepper.

4. To serve, stir the ingredients in the slow cooker and transfer to serving plates. Serve with rice, potatoes, or toast.

Venison Tenderloin Sandwiches

If you're looking to make friends using your deer harvest, this sandwich recipe is a tried-and-true crowd pleaser. Many hunters mistakenly refer to the loins (or backstraps) as tenderloins; the tenderloins are the flattish strips located on the inside of the spine. Get really good rolls from your local bakery to make the sandwiches extra special.

Makes: 4 sandwiches

Prep Time: 5 minutes

Cook Time: 15 minutes

Ingredients

- » 2 cups mushrooms, sliced
- » ¼ cup butter
- » ¼ cup Worcestershire sauce
- » Eight 12-ounce venison tenderloin steaks
- » ½ teaspoon garlic powder
- » ½ teaspoon salt
- » ¼ teaspoon pepper
- » 4 large, hard rolls

Preparation

1. In a large skillet over medium heat, sauté the onions and mushrooms in the butter and Worcestershire sauce.

2. Meanwhile, pound each venison steak to a thickness of about ½ inch. Add the tenderloins to the skillet. Cook the steaks for approximately 4 to 5 minutes on each side or to your desired doneness. Sprinkle the garlic powder, salt, and pepper over the steaks while they are cooking.

3. To serve, split each hard roll in half and set the rolls open-faced on a plate. Place 2 steaks on the bottom half of each roll. Place a generous amount of the sautéed onions and mushrooms over each sandwich. Replace the top half of each roll and serve with any remaining sautéed onions or mushrooms on the side.

Tenderloins have a flat, even shape that allows for more uniform cooking and seasoning.

A smoker is needed to get the perfect flavor.

Spiced Wine Venison Sausage

This is a good starter recipe for people who like game sausage with a twist. You will need a meat grinder or stuffer and sausage casings to make the sausages. This sausage stuffing mix also works well in a tomatoey red sauce served over pasta.

Makes: About 15 servings

Prep Time: 15 minutes, plus 4 days chilling

Cook Time: 4 to 6 hours

Ingredients

» 3½ pounds ground venison
» 1½ pounds lard or beef tallow
» 3½ tablespoons tenderizing salt
» ¾ cup Burgundy wine
» 2 tablespoons sugar
» 2 tablespoons mustard seed
» 1 tablespoon onion powder
» 1 ½ teaspoons coriander
» 1 ½ teaspoons minced fresh ginger
» ½ teaspoon ground nutmeg
» 1 ½ teaspoons garlic powder
» 1 ½ teaspoons pepper
» Sausage casings, as needed

Preparation

1. In a large bowl, combine the ground venison, lard or tallow, and tenderizing salt, mixing thoroughly by hand for 5 minutes. Cover the bowl and chill it in the refrigerator for 3 days, mixing twice each day.

2. On the fourth day, in a medium bowl, combine the wine, sugar, mustard seed, onion powder, coriander, ginger, nutmeg, garlic powder, and pepper and mix well. Add the wine mixture to the meat and mix until well combined.

3. Stuff the mixture into the sausage casings. Using a smoker, smoke the sausages over hickory chips at 160°F for 4 hours. Increase the temperature to 180°F and continue to smoke until the sausage reaches 160°F on a meat thermometer. Chill the sausages in the refrigerator for 24 hours before slicing and serving.

Venison Jerky

The USDA recommends that jerky made from venison first be steamed, roasted, or boiled to 160°F before drying. Jerky can be made in a smoker, dehydrator, or your oven—instructions for all three methods are given here. If using the oven, place a foil ball between the oven door and the body of the oven so that the evaporating liquids can escape. The idea is to remove as much of the liquid as possible from the meat. For storage, vacuum-seal or place in freezer-safe bags and freeze for up to 1 year.

Ingredients
» Venison, as needed

Makes: approximately ¼ lb. for every 1 lb. venison used
Prep Time: 15 minutes, plus 12 to 24 hours marinating
Cook Time: 1 to 10 hours

Preparation

1. Cut your venison into long, even, thin strips. Then steam, roast, or boil the strips until they reach 160°F. Allow the meat to cool.

2. In a medium bowl, combine the liquid and/or marinade ingredients of your choice (see page 33). Add the venison strips and mix until the strips are completely covered in marinade or seasonings. Cover the bowl and place it in the refrigerator for 12 to 24 hours to marinate.

3. Remove the meat, discard the marinade, and allow the meat to air-dry for 30 minutes before processing in the dehydrator, oven, or smoker.

4a. **Using a Dehydrator:** Set the dehydrator to 160°F. Place the marinated venison strips on the dehydrator racks and close the dehydrator tightly. Turn on the dehydrator and dry the strips for 8 to 10 hours, turning at least once halfway through.

4b. **Using the Oven:** Remove all oven racks and place one rack in the lowest position in the oven. Set a large baking sheet on the lowest rack. Preheat the oven to 200°F. Using toothpicks and one of the removed oven racks, create hanging supports for the venison strips: Drape the marinated strips over the toothpicks and suspend the toothpicks between the bars of the rack. Return the rack to the oven. Cook for 2 to 3 hours, sampling for desired doneness after every hour.

4c. **Using a Grill or Smoker:** Cook the marinated venison strips at 200°F over indirect heat for 1 to 2 hours, sampling for desired doneness every 30 minutes.

Jerky Marinades

There are nine recipes for venison jerky marinades in the following pages, and all of them follow the simple instructions given here. Experiment, have fun, and try out as many of them as you can!

1. Combine all the marinade ingredients in a large saucepan over low heat, stirring, and allow the flavors to blend.

2. Allow the marinade to cool completely before adding the venison strips.

Basic Jerky Marinade

» ⅓ cup garlic salt
» ⅓ cup onion salt
» ⅓ cup pepper
» ⅓ cup salt
» 1 cup Worcestershire sauce

Smoky

» 1 tablespoon liquid smoke flavoring
» ¾ cup soy sauce
» ¾ cup Worcestershire sauce
» 3 tablespoons ketchup
» ¾ teaspoon garlic powder
» ¾ teaspoon salt
» ¼ to ½ teaspoons pepper

Western BBQ

» 1 cup red wine vinegar
» 1 cup ketchup
» 6 tablespoons brown sugar
» 1 tablespoon onion powder
» 1 tablespoon dry mustard powder
» 1 tablespoon salt
» 1 ½ teaspoons garlic powder
» ¾ teaspoon pepper
» ½ teaspoon cayenne pepper

Kickin' Spiced

» 1 cup soy sauce
» ½ cup lime juice
» ½ cup vinegar
» ¼ cup crushed red pepper flakes
» 2 tablespoons garlic powder

Baja Style

» 2 tablespoons salt
» 2 tablespoons pepper
» 2 tablespoons coriander
» 1 ½ teaspoons chili powder
» 1 ½ teaspoons ground ginger
» 1 ½ teaspoons ground turmeric
» 1 ½ teaspoons ground cumin

Mild Mexican

» 1 tablespoon salt
» 1 tablespoon chili powder
» 1 tablespoon paprika
» 1 ½ teaspoons garlic powder
» 1 ½ teaspoons dried oregano
» ¾ teaspoon pepper

Spicy Garlic

» 6 garlic cloves, minced
» ½ cup Worcestershire sauce
» 6 tablespoons tangy barbecue sauce
» 1 tablespoon onion powder
» 1 tablespoon salt
» 1 ½ teaspoons paprika
» ¾ teaspoon cracked peppercorns
» ¾ teaspoon cayenne pepper

Asian

» 1 large onion, minced
» 5 garlic cloves, pressed
» 1 ½ cups pineapple juice
» 1 ¼ cups red wine
» ⅓ cup soy sauce
» 1 cup brown sugar
» 2 tablespoons salt
» 2 tablespoons pepper
» 1 tablespoon peeled and minced fresh ginger

Tangy

» 1 small onion, minced
» ½ cup lemon juice
» ¼ cup brown sugar
» 3 bay leaves, crushed
» 1 tablespoon seasoned salt
» 2 teaspoons liquid smoke flavoring
» ¼ teaspoon pepper

Different marinades will change the flavor of your homemade jerky.

Grilled Elk Chops

What some folks call a "chop" could be any trimmed portion from the loin of an animal. Whether you leave the rib bone attached is optional. Overcooking is not an option if you want your cooked chops to be tender and delicious, so tune in and be an attentive grill master. This dish gives you your best chance to show off not only your grilling skills but also your skill as a big game hunter.

Makes: 8 to 10 servings
Prep Time: 10 minutes
Cook Time: 25 to 35 minutes

Ingredients

» 10 elk chops, trimmed of visible fat
» 1 large onion
» 4 garlic cloves
» 6 ounces beer
» ¼ cup butter or margarine
» Salt and pepper, to taste

Preparation

1. Use disposable aluminum foil pans or create your own using a double layer of heavy-duty foil and molding it over an upside-down pan or large rectangular baking dish; leave extra at all edges, fold them over, and crimp them well for strength. Preheat an outdoor grill to medium-high heat.

2. Place the elk chops in the pans. Chop the onion and mince the garlic. Sprinkle the onion and garlic over the elk chops. Pour the beer over the chops. Cut the butter into pats and place one on top of each of the chops. Place the pan on the grate and cover the grill.

3. Cook for 8 to 10 minutes then remove them from the pan. The elk chops will still be rare.

4. Discard the pan and all the drippings. Return the elk chops to the hot grill and sprinkle them with salt and pepper. Grill for 2 minutes on each side, or until they are evenly marked. A medium-rare elk chop will be about 130–135°F in the center.

Chops can include the bone or not. The bone can help retain some moisture in the meat and many prefer the style of a bone-in presentation.

Elk & Pepper Stir-Fry

Cooking trimmed, sliced elk in a wok or skillet happens quickly, so be attentive at your station. The finished elk should be tender and just cooked, not overcooked, or the meat can be tough and chewy. If your stir-fried elk isn't tender, don't blame the elk. The stir-fry flavors provide a rich fullness that will suit any diner who is skeptical of elk meat.

Ingredients

» One 1-pound elk steak, thinly sliced across the grain
» ½ cup soy sauce, plus more as needed
» 2 tablespoons cornstarch, divided
» ½ cup peanut oil, divided
» 4 medium tomatoes
» 1 green bell pepper
» ¾ cup chicken broth, divided
» ¼ cup sweet chili sauce
» Rice, cooked, to serve (optional)

Makes: 4 servings

Prep Time: 15 minutes,
   plus 30 minutes
      to 24 hours marinating

Cook Time: 15 minutes

Preparation

1. Place the sliced elk meat in a large bowl. Pour the soy sauce over the elk and sprinkle with half the cornstarch; mix lightly. Cover the bowl and place it in the refrigerator for at least 30 minutes and up to 24 hours to marinate.

2. Remove the elk from the refrigerator and discard the marinade. Place ¼ cup peanut oil in a large skillet over medium-high heat. Once the oil is hot, place the elk strips in the skillet and cook, stirring often, until the strips are browned on all sides, but still rare. Remove the strips and drippings and set aside.

3. Meanwhile, chop the tomatoes and cut the pepper into thin strips. Add the other ¼ cup peanut oil to the skillet over medium-high heat. Add the tomatoes and heat for 1 minute, stirring constantly. Place 1 tablespoon of the chicken broth in a small glass and set aside. Add the remaining chicken broth to the skillet. Stir in the pepper strips and cooked elk strips with drippings in the skillet. Mix in the sweet chili sauce and stir well.

4. Add the remaining cornstarch to the chicken broth in the small glass and mix well. Push the steak and vegetables to one side of the skillet and slowly pour the cornstarch mixture into the liquid in the pan. Mix lightly and bring the mixture to a boil to thicken, stirring constantly. Mix all ingredients together, adding more soy sauce as desired. If desired, serve over hot cooked rice.

Asian-inspired flavors elevate the elk meat flavors.

Crunchy cornbread on top of warm, soft casserole makes this a comfort dish for friends and family.

Skillet Cornbread Elk Casserole

This satisfying comfort dish is easy to make—hunting the elk is the hard part—as it uses everyday pantry ingredients. Try making this in a Dutch oven at your next campout. If you don't want to use fresh corn, substitute canned whole kernel corn.

Makes: 4 to 6 servings
Prep Time: 10 minutes
Cook Time: 30 minutes

Ingredients

» 8 to 10 bacon strips
» 1 medium onion
» 2 pounds ground elk meat
» 2 cups fresh corn kernels
» Two 10¾-ounce cans tomato soup
» 1 teaspoon garlic powder
» One 1¼-ounce package chili seasoning
» Two 8½-ounce boxes corn muffin mix
» 1 egg
» ⅓ cup milk

Preparation

1. Preheat the oven to 350°F. In a large skillet over medium-high heat, cook the bacon strips to your desired crispiness. Remove the bacon strips and place them on paper towels to drain, reserving the drippings in the skillet. Crumble the cooked bacon.

2. Chop the onion. Add the onion and elk meat to the drippings in the skillet. Heat, stirring often, until the onions are tender and the meat is browned. Pour the drippings from the skillet, retaining the onions and meat in the skillet. Reduce the heat to medium. Add the corn, tomato soup, garlic powder, chili seasoning, and bacon to the skillet.

3. In a medium bowl, combine the corn muffin mix, egg, and milk. Mix until well combined. Spread the cornbread batter over the ingredients in the skillet. Place the skillet in the oven and bake for 15 to 20 minutes, or until the cornbread topping is golden brown.

Perfect Pulled Feral Hog

Feral swine are populating southern states faster than they can be harvested by hunters so if you have access to hunting areas down there you have a good chance of coming back from the hunt with boar meat to spare. Wild boar hunters understand that there is a world of difference in taste and texture between an old male boar and a young female. That big boar head might look cool on your wall, but the younger ones make much better table fare. This method turns any feral swine, large or small, into moist, shredded morsels. You can make this recipe with the bone in or out.

Ingredients

- » ¼ cup brown sugar
- » ¼ cup kosher salt
- » ¼ cup paprika
- » 2 tablespoons black pepper
- » 2 tablespoons onion powder
- » 2 tablespoons garlic powder
- » 1 tablespoon cayenne pepper
- » 1 wild hog shoulder or hindquarter roast
- » 2 cups barbecue sauce

Makes: 8 to 10 servings

Prep Time: 10 minutes, plus 6 hours rub

Cook Time: 6 to 8 hours

Preparation

1. Combine the rub ingredients—the sugar and dry spices—and evenly coat the roast with the mixed rub. Wrap the rubbed roast with plastic wrap and refrigerate it for 6 to 48 hours.

2. Smoke, roast, or grill (covered) at 250°F for 6 to 8 hours, or until the internal temperature away from the bone is 180°F. If desired, first brown the roast evenly in a hot oven or on a hot grill. This will give the roast additional flavor and extra crunch on the edges.

3. Place the roast on top of two or three long sheets of heavy-duty foil. Pour the barbecue sauce over the roast and wrap it snugly with foil so that sauce will not run out. Place the roast back in the 250°F oven, smoker, or grill and cook for another 2 hours.

4. Remove the roast and allow it to cool enough to handle. Shred the meat with your fingers, tongs, or forks.

Letting the rub sit for up to two days will enhance the flavor.

Trout & Salmon

You can do a lot with fish like trout and salmon, from nicer dishes to cozy homestyle meals.

Americans eat trout of all colors and sizes, and they are some of the most popular U.S. game fish, enjoyed by small stream fly fishermen to deep water trophy fishermen. Trout are mild in flavor, especially the larger lake trout, which can also be somewhat soft in texture. Mountain stream-caught trout are best cooked right away over a campfire. Finished with a squeeze of lemon or lime and a chunk of butter, they are a fitting end to a great day on the water. Don't waste the tasty flesh by filleting small trout before cooking. After they are cooked, the skeleton can be easily removed and discarded, leaving the cooked fillets on the plate. Larger trout can be stuffed with vegetables, butter, and citrus fruits before securing with string or skewers and roasted, grilled, or baked. As with any fish, drizzling fresh lemon juice over the cooked fish right before serving will make the fish come deliciously alive.

Over 70 percent of the salmon consumed in the United States is farmed, but that's not necessarily bad news. Our oceans cannot support the demand for seafood, so farmed fish is a big part of the future. Wild-caught salmon are firmer and denser in flavor than farmed, but some populations along the West Coast haven't been sustainable, so regulating agencies have had to restrict harvesting of wild fish. When shopping for salmon at the market, find out where the fish is from. In the U.S., fish markets must label their catch with their "Country of Origin." Not all fish farms are the same. Do some research and find out where the best salmon are responsibly raised. Salmon that is just-cooked will be moist and flavorful. Overcooked salmon will be more fishy and dry.

Green onions are also a good topping option for this dish.

Grilled Steelhead with Pickled Cucumbers

This steelhead is seasoned with just enough heat to balance the cool, crisp cucumbers. Pickling your own summer-fresh cucumbers gives you a great way to use your garden harvest as well as your catch to delicious effect. This recipe works just as well with other grilled trout species or with salmon.

Makes: 2 servings

Prep Time: 20 to 25 minutes

Cook Time: 12 to 16 minutes

Ingredients

Pickled Cucumbers

» ¼ cup white vinegar
» ¼ cup sugar
» ½ teaspoon salt
» ½ yellow onion, peeled and thinly sliced
» 1 large cucumber, thinly sliced

Fillets

» Two 6- to 8-ounce steelhead fillets, skin intact
» Juice of 2 lemons
» 2 tablespoons vegetable oil
» 1 teaspoon freshly ground black pepper
» ½ teaspoon sea salt
» Asian chili-garlic sauce, to taste, for topping
» 1 teaspoon toasted sesame seeds, for topping

Preparation

1. **Prepare the Pickled Cucumbers.** In a saucepan over medium heat, combine ½ cup of water and all of the ingredients, except the onion and cucumber, and cook, stirring, until the sugar is dissolved. Do not boil. Place the cucumber and onion in a bowl, pour the liquid over top, and chill the mixture in the refrigerator for 2 to 3 hours.

2. Lay the fillets, skin side down, in a shallow tray or dish and squeeze lemon juice over top. Rub oil over the fillets then season with pepper and salt. Cover and refrigerate for 1 hour.

3. Remove the Pickled Cucumbers from the refrigerator and set aside. Place the fillets, skin side down, on a grill grate at medium-low. Cover and cook for 6 to 7 minutes. Carefully turn the fillets one-quarter turn on the grate, keeping the skin side down. Replace the cover and cook 4 to 5 minutes more. The fish should be firm to the touch and light pink in color.

4. Drain the Pickled Cucumbers well and arrange them on plates. Remove the fillets from the grill. Carefully remove the skin and place them on top of the cucumbers and top with a drizzle of the Asian chili-garlic sauce and garnish with toasted sesame seeds.

Ginger-Lime Grilled Trout

With the sauce, you get just enough spicy heat, lime, and ginger to get your attention, but not so much that you can't appreciate the flavor of the trout.

Makes: 4 servings
Prep Time: 10 minutes
Cook Time: 4 to 8 minutes

Ingredients

» ¼ cup safflower oil, plus more as needed
» 1 tablespoon fresh ginger, peeled and grated
» ½ teaspoon crushed red pepper flakes
» 2 tablespoons freshly squeezed lime juice
» 1 teaspoon lime zest
» Four ½-pound trout fillets
» Salt and pepper, to taste

Preparation

1. Warm the safflower oil in a small saucepan over medium-high heat. Add the ginger to the hot oil and sauté until just lightly browned and fragrant. Remove the saucepan from heat and stir in the crushed red pepper flakes. When the oil has cooled completely, gradually whisk in the lime juice and lime zest. Mix well and set aside.

2. Preheat the grill to high heat and lightly oil the grate. Season the trout fillets with salt and pepper to taste. Once the grill is hot, grill the trout, flesh side down, for 2 to 4 minutes. Gently turn the fillets over and grill for 2 to 4 additional minutes or until the fish turns opaque.

3. To serve, immediately transfer the grilled trout to serving plates. Drizzle the lime and ginger mixture over each fillet and serve.

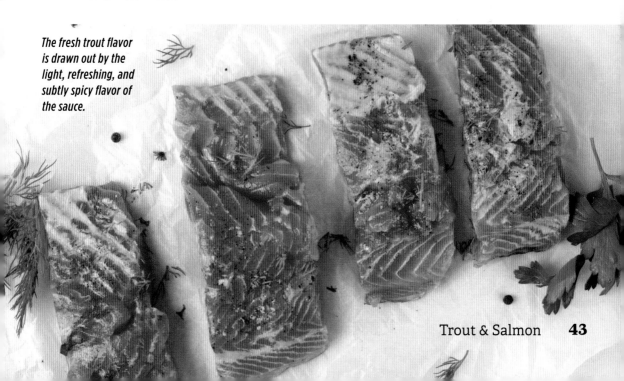

The fresh trout flavor is drawn out by the light, refreshing, and subtly spicy flavor of the sauce.

Asian-Inspired Salmon Steaks

Assertive Asian flavors—ginger with soy and orange juice concentrate—complement this versatile fish. If you like a little heat to balance the sweet, add a minced jalapeño or a dash of Asian sweet chili sauce.

Makes: 4 servings

Prep Time: 15 minutes, plus 1 hour marinating

Cook Time: 6 to 10 minutes

Ingredients

Ginger Marinade

» 1 to 2 green onions
» 1 clove garlic
» One ½-inch piece ginger
» ⅓ cup soy sauce
» ¼ cup orange juice concentrate
» 2 tablespoons vegetable oil
» 2 tablespoons tomato sauce (optional)
» 1 teaspoon freshly squeezed lemon juice
» ½ teaspoon yellow mustard

Steaks

» Four ½-pound salmon steaks, about 1-inch thick
» 1 tablespoon olive oil, plus more as needed

Preparation

1. **Prepare the Ginger Marinade.** Chop the green onions and mince the garlic. Mince or finely grate the ginger. In a small bowl, combine the green onions, garlic, ginger, soy sauce, orange juice concentrate, vegetable oil, tomato sauce (if using), lemon juice, and mustard. Mix everything together until well combined.

2. Place the salmon steaks in an even layer in a 9 x 13–inch glass baking dish. Pour the Ginger Marinade over the salmon, turning to coat both sides. Cover the baking dish with plastic wrap and place it in the refrigerator for 1 hour to marinate, turning the steaks over after 30 minutes.

3. Preheat an outdoor grill to high heat and lightly oil the grate. Remove the baking dish from the refrigerator. Pour the marinade into a small saucepan and place the saucepan over high heat; boil for 1 minute.

4. Using a pastry brush, brush the salmon steaks lightly with olive oil. Grill the steaks for 3 to 5 minutes on one side. Gently turn the steaks over and grill for an additional 3 to 5 minutes. Brush the marinade over the salmon as it is grilling. The salmon is done when it flakes easily with a fork. Discard any remaining marinade. Transfer the grilled salmon to a serving dish and serve immediately.

Try putting some of your favorite steamed or roasted veggies on the side of this dish.

Parsley is another great topper for lemon-grilled salmon.

Lemon-Grilled Salmon

After shrimp, salmon is the most popular seafood in the United States, and for good reason. This delicious fish is loaded with high levels of healthy omega-3 fatty acids and is an excellent source of protein. Prepare the fish with the skin on or off, to your preference.

Makes: 6 to 8 servings

Prep Time: 15 minutes, plus 1 hour marinating

Cook Time: 15 to 20 minutes

Ingredients

Marinade
- » 2 to 3 green onions
- » ¼ cups brown sugar
- » 3 tablespoons olive oil
- » 3 tablespoons soy sauce
- » ¼ cup freshly squeezed lemon juice

Fillets
- » 1 tablespoon minced fresh dill
- » ½ teaspoon pepper
- » ½ teaspoon salt
- » ¼ teaspoon garlic powder
- » 1½ to 2 pounds salmon fillets
- » Oil, as needed
- » 4 lemons, halved

Preparation

1. In a small bowl, combine the dill, pepper, salt, and garlic powder and mix well. Sprinkle the seasoning mixture over all sides of the salmon fillets. Place the seasoned fillets in a large resealable plastic bag or shallow glass dish.

2. **Prepare the Marinade.** Finely chop the green onions. In a medium bowl, combine the green onions, brown sugar, olive oil, soy sauce, and lemon juice and mix until evenly blended. Pour the Marinade over the salmon in the bag or dish. Seal the bag, or cover the dish with plastic wrap, and place it in the refrigerator for 1 hour to marinate, turning the fillets over after 30 minutes.

3. Preheat an outdoor grill to medium heat and lightly oil the grate. Remove the salmon from the refrigerator and discard the Marinade. Once the grill is hot, place the salmon, skin side down (if intact), on the grill. Place the lemon halves, cut side down, on the grill. Grill the lemons for 3 to 4 minutes, then give them a quarter turn for diamond-pattern grill marks.

4. Cover the grill with the lid or a foil pan and cook for 12 to 15 minutes or until the salmon flakes easily with a fork. Do not turn the salmon over while grilling. Serve immediately with a grilled lemon half on the side.

Almond Trout

A simple preparation for one of America's favorite culinary fishes, this recipe works just as well in the home kitchen as it does streamside cooked over white-hot coals, though, in the latter case, the effort to reach the point where the meal can be enjoyed makes it taste that much better.

Makes: 2 servings
Prep Time: 15 minutes
Cook Time: 15 minutes

Ingredients

» Two ½- to 1-pound pieces of trout, dressed
» Salt and pepper, to taste
» ¼ cup flour
» 4 tablespoons butter, divided
» ½ cups blanched, slivered almonds
» 2 tablespoons freshly squeezed lemon juice
» 1 lemon, to serve
» 1 tablespoon chopped fresh parsley, to serve

Sauté the almonds until they are light brown.

Preparation

1. Rinse the trout and pat it dry with paper towels. Season the inside and outside of the trout with salt and pepper to taste. Place the flour in a large pie plate and dredge the trout in the flour.

2. Place 2 tablespoons of butter in a large skillet over high heat. Once the butter is melted, add the trout to the skillet and cook, turning once, until it is browned on both sides. Reduce the heat to medium and continue to cook for about 5 minutes on each side or until the fish flakes easily with a fork. Remove the trout from the pan and set aside, keeping it warm in the oven.

3. Quickly wipe out the skillet with a wet paper towel and add the remaining 2 tablespoons of butter. Place the skillet over medium heat just until the butter begins to brown. Add the almonds and sauté them until they are lightly brown. Drizzle the butter and almond sauce over the fish. Sprinkle the lemon juice lightly over the fish.

4. Cut the lemon into slices. Garnish the fish with the lemon slices and chopped fresh parsley. Serve immediately.

Blackened Salmon with Tomato Relish

This recipe is best cooked in a white-hot cast-iron skillet. Blackening fish is a smoky, splattery ordeal, and the fumes can make breathing a chore, so make sure the windows are open and there's plenty of ventilation. If you can prepare this dish outdoors, do so. To avoid burning your fingers, do not touch the pan for at least an hour after the heat has been turned off.

Ingredients

Tomato Relish

- » 2 cups peeled, seeded, and diced tomato
- » ¼ cup red onion
- » 3 garlic cloves, minced
- » ⅓ cup pitted chopped black olives
- » ¼ cup minced fresh basil or Italian parsley
- » 1 teaspoon lemon juice
- » ½ teaspoon Dijon mustard
- » 3 tablespoons balsamic vinegar
- » Pinch sugar
- » 3 tablespoons olive oil
- » Salt and pepper, to taste

Blackening Spice Mix

- » ½ teaspoon freshly ground black pepper
- » ½ teaspoon white pepper
- » ½ teaspoon cayenne pepper
- » ½ teaspoon dried oregano leaves
- » ¼ teaspoon ground oregano
- » ¼ teaspoon ground thyme
- » 1 tablespoon paprika
- » 1 teaspoon garlic powder
- » 1 teaspoon onion powder
- » 2 teaspoons salt

Fillets

- » Four 6- to 8-ounce salmon fillets, skin removed, about 1 inch thick
- » Pan coating spray, as needed
- » ¼ cup sour cream, for topping

Makes: 4 servings

Prep Time: 10 minutes

Cook Time: 8 to 10 minutes

Preparation

1. **Prepare the Tomato Relish.** In a bowl, combine the tomato with the red onion, garlic, olives and basil or parsley. In another bowl, combine the lemon juice, mustard, vinegar, and sugar. While whisking the lemon juice mixture, add olive oil in a thin stream to emulsify. Season with salt and pepper and add the lemon juice mixture to the bowl with the tomato mixture. Set aside and allow it to rest at room temperature for 30 to 60 minutes.

2. Heat a cast-iron or other heavy skillet over high heat until it is extremely hot, about 20 minutes.

3. **Prepare the Blackening Spice Mix.** In a medium bowl, combine all the ingredients and mix well. Set aside.

4. Lightly spray each side of the fillets with pan spray. Season the fillets evenly with the Blackening Spice Mix. Place the fish, 1 or 2 at a time, in the skillet for 1 to 2 minutes per side or until they are seared on each side. The fish should be crisp on the outside and moist on the inside. Check the first piece for doneness and adjust the cooking time accordingly for the remaining pieces.

5. Top each fillet with a spoonful of Tomato Relish and a dollop of sour cream.

Colorful vegetables on the side contrast against the blackened salmon both in brightness and temperature to create a perfect balance.

Garlic-Marinated Baked Salmon

A sumptuous marinade that combines freshly squeezed lemon juice, olive oil, basil, parsley, and pepper brings all the best qualities of salmon to the fore when it is baked. Treat yourself and your guests to one of our most traditional, delectable wild-caught dishes. Pair with a white wine to reach next-level goodness.

Ingredients

» 2 garlic cloves
» 6 tablespoons olive oil
» 1 teaspoon dried basil
» 1 teaspoon salt
» 1 teaspoon pepper
» 1 tablespoon lemon juice
» 1 tablespoon chopped fresh parsley
» Two ½-pound salmon fillets

Makes: 2 servings

Prep Time: 15 minutes, plus 1 hour marinating

Cook Time: 35 to 45 minutes

Preparation

1. Mince the garlic. In a medium glass bowl, combine the garlic, olive oil, basil, salt, pepper, lemon juice, and parsley.

2. Place the salmon fillets, skin side up, in a 9-inch-square glass baking dish. Pour the garlic marinade mixture evenly over the salmon fillets. Cover the baking dish with plastic wrap and place it in the refrigerator for 1 hour to marinate, turning the salmon fillets over after 30 minutes.

3. Preheat the oven to 375°F. Tear off one sheet of aluminum foil large enough to wrap around the salmon fillets. Remove the salmon from the refrigerator. Place the fillets on the aluminum foil. Pour the marinade into a small saucepan over high heat and bring it to a boil for 1 minute. Pour the hot marinade over the salmon fillets. Wrap the aluminum foil up and over the salmon, sealing the edges. Place the wrapped fillets in a glass baking dish. Bake for 35 to 45 minutes or until the salmon flakes easily with a fork.

4. To serve, remove the baking dish from the oven and carefully unwrap the aluminum foil packet. Transfer each fillet to a serving plate and serve immediately.

Letting the salmon marinate for 45 minutes will solidify the flavors.

The dish works well without sauce (as pictured), though sauce will bring it to the next level.

Pan-Fried Trout in Pecan Sauce

If pecans aren't readily available, try this with any other nut. Whatever nut you choose for the sauce, make sure to roast them before preparing the sauce. Pecans give it a smoky, sweet, Southern flavor.

Makes: 6 to 8 servings

*Prep Time: 15 minutes, plus
    1 hour marinating*

Cook Time: 15 to 20 minutes

Ingredients

Pecan Sauce

» ½ cup pecan halves
» 2 green onions
» 1 clove garlic
» ¼ cup butter, softened
» 1 teaspoon lemon juice
» ⅛ teaspoon lemon zest
» ½ teaspoon hot pepper sauce

Fillets

» Four ½-pound trout fillets
» ¼ cup flour
» 2 tablespoons finely ground pecans
» ¾ teaspoon salt
» ¼ teaspoon white pepper
» Pinch cayenne pepper
» 2 tablespoons vegetable oil
» ¼ cup butter

Preparation

1. **Begin by preparing the Pecan Sauce.** Preheat the oven to 350°F. Arrange the pecan halves in an even layer on a baking sheet. Bake the pecans for 8 minutes or until lightly browned. Coarsely chop the green onions and mince the garlic. In a blender, combine the toasted pecans, green onions, garlic, butter, lemon juice, lemon zest, and hot pepper sauce. Process the mixture on high until well blended and smooth; set aside.

2. Rinse the trout fillets and pat them dry with paper towels. In a medium bowl, combine the flour, ground pecans, salt, white pepper, and cayenne pepper. Dredge the fillets in the flour mixture, turning to coat both sides.

3. Meanwhile, place the vegetable oil and butter in a large skillet over medium-high heat. Once the butter is melted, place the trout fillets in the skillet and fry for 2 to 4 minutes per side or until the coating is golden brown. Remove the trout and set them aside on paper towels to drain.

4. To serve, place the fried trout fillets on a serving dish and spread a generous 2 tablespoons of the pecan sauce over each fillet.

Broiled Trout

If the weather is hot and you want to keep it cool in the kitchen, try this on the outside grill instead. If the grill doesn't have a cover, place a foil pan over the grilling fish.

Ingredients

- » Four to six ½- to 1-pound whole trout, cleaned and scaled
- » 2 tablespoons butter
- » 1 clove garlic
- » ½ small onion
- » ½ small green bell pepper
- » One 8-ounce can tomato sauce
- » 2 tablespoons lemon juice
- » 1 tablespoon Worcestershire sauce
- » 1 tablespoon brown sugar
- » ½ teaspoon chili powder
- » 2 tablespoons freshly squeezed lemon juice

Makes: 4 to 6 servings

Prep Time: 15 minutes, plus 30 minutes marinating

Cook Time: 10 to 16 minutes

Preparation

1. Cut the cleaned and scaled trout into serving-size portions and place them in a single layer in a 9 x 13–inch glass baking dish.

2. Place the butter in a large skillet over medium-high heat. Mince the garlic and chop the onion and green pepper. Once the butter is melted, sauté the garlic, onion, and green pepper until the onion is softened. Stir in the tomato sauce, lemon juice, Worcestershire sauce, brown sugar, and chili powder. Bring the mixture to a simmer and cook for 5 minutes, stirring occasionally. Remove the skillet from heat and let it cool. Once it has cooled, pour the sauce over the fish in the baking dish. Cover and place the baking dish in the refrigerator for 30 minutes to marinate, turning the fish after 15 minutes.

3. Preheat the oven broiler to high heat and grease a sheet pan well. Remove the fish from the marinade, reserving the marinade, and place the fish on the sheet pan. Transfer the marinade to a medium saucepan over medium-high heat. Bring the marinade to a rolling boil for 5 minutes then remove it from heat. Broil the fish about 4 inches from the heat for 5 to 8 minutes. Baste the fish with the boiled marinade. Turn the fish over and broil for an additional 5 to 8 minutes or until the fish flakes easily with a fork.

Broiling the trout will get it to perfect flakiness.

4. To serve, transfer the grilled or broiled fish to a serving dish and sprinkle with 2 tablespoons of lemon juice.

Baked Stuffed Trout

Paired with a salad and a glass of chardonnay, you will want to make this a regular meal all year long, especially if you've had good luck in the trout stream and hungry guests to impress.

Makes: 8 servings
Prep Time: 30 minutes
Cook Time: 20 minutes

Ingredients

- » Eight ½- to 1-pound whole trout
- » 8 slices stale bread
- » 1 small onion
- » 2 celery stalks
- » ¼ cup butter, plus ½ cup, melted
- » 2 teaspoons minced garlic
- » 1 cup chicken or fish broth
- » 2 teaspoons chopped fresh thyme
- » 2 teaspoons salt
- » 1 teaspoon pepper
- » ½ teaspoon hot pepper sauce
- » 3 tablespoons freshly squeezed lemon juice

Preparation

1. Gut the trout, removing the heads and tails. Rinse the inside and outside of each fish and pat them dry with paper towels. Cut or tear the stale bread into 1-inch pieces and place them in a medium bowl; set the bowl aside. Chop the onion and dice the celery.

2. Preheat the oven to 350°F. Place ¼ cup of butter in a large skillet over medium heat. Once the butter is melted, add the onion, celery, and garlic and sauté until the onions just begin to turn brown.

3. Add the chicken broth, thyme, salt, and pepper to the onion mixture in the skillet and mix well. Add the hot pepper sauce and simmer for 2 to 3 minutes. Pour the mixture over the bread pieces in the bowl and toss until the bread is completely moistened. Divide the stuffing into 8 portions. Stuff each trout evenly with one of the stuffing portions and secure with toothpicks. Place the stuffed trout in two 9 x 13–inch glass baking dishes. Bake for 20 minutes or until the fish flakes easily with a fork.

4. Meanwhile, combine the ½ cup of melted butter and the lemon juice in a small bowl. To serve, transfer the baked trout to a serving dish and carefully remove the toothpicks. Drizzle the stuffed trout with the melted butter mixture and serve.

Baked stuffed trout is a great dish no matter the time of year.

While this dish calls for the whole trout, you can adjust for your comfort level.

Baked Whole Trout

This steelhead is seasoned with just enough heat to balance the cool, crisp cucumbers. Pickling your own summer-fresh cucumbers gives you a great way to use your garden harvest as well as your catch to delicious effect. This recipe works just as well with other grilled trout species or with salmon.

Ingredients

» Six ½- to 1-pound whole trout
» 1 onion
» 3 ounces fresh mushrooms
» 1 teaspoon chopped fresh parsley
» ½ teaspoon salt, plus more to taste
» Pepper, to taste
» ½ teaspoon dried tarragon

» 2 tablespoons butter, melted
» 4 egg yolks
» 3 tablespoons brandy
» ⅛ teaspoon white pepper
» ½ cup dry breadcrumbs
» ½ cup shredded Swiss cheese
» ⅛ teaspoon paprika

Makes: 6 servings
Prep Time: 10 to 15 minutes
Cook Time: 15 minutes

Preparation

1. Gut the trout but leave the heads and tails intact.

2. Preheat the oven to 400°F. Lightly grease a 9 x 13–inch glass baking dish. Finely chop the onion and mushrooms. Place the onion and mushrooms in an even layer across the bottom of the baking dish. Sprinkle the parsley and salt and pepper, to taste, over the onions and mushrooms.

3. Arrange the trout over the vegetables. Sprinkle the tarragon over the fish and drizzle with the melted butter. Cover the baking dish with aluminum foil. Bake for 10 minutes.

4. Meanwhile, in a small bowl, combine the egg yolks, brandy, ½ teaspoon of salt, and the white pepper. Remove the foil from the baking dish and pour the egg mixture evenly over the fish. Sprinkle the breadcrumbs, Swiss cheese, and paprika over the trout. Return the baking dish to the oven for 5 minutes or until the fish flakes easily with a fork and the breadcrumbs are lightly browned.

5. To serve, place one whole baked trout on each serving plate. Drizzle the sauce, onions, and mushrooms from the pan over each serving.

Salmon with Shrimp Topping

Salmon's high oil content and assertive flavors work well with this bold stuffing mixture, which marries anchovies, shrimp, and mushrooms. The stuffing mixture is also great for stuffing whole fish like trout. You can prepare the salmon with the skin on or off, to your preference.

Ingredients

Fillets

» Four 6-ounce salmon fillets
» ½ teaspoon salt, plus more to taste
» Pinch black pepper, plus more to taste
» 1 tablespoon lemon juice
» Butter, as needed
» 4 strips bacon, cut in half, partially cooked
» 1 cup white wine

Stuffing

» 4 green onions
» 6 mushrooms
» 2 tablespoons butter
» 2 tablespoons minced fresh parsley
» 6 anchovies (optional)
» 10 raw medium shrimp, peeled and deveined
» ⅓ cup dry breadcrumbs

Makes: 4 servings

Prep Time:
15 minutes, plus
45 minutes chilling

Cook Time: 45 minutes

Preparation

1. Pat the salmon fillets gently with dry paper towels. Season with salt and pepper and brush each fillet with lemon juice. Preheat the oven to 375°F.

2. **Prepare the Stuffing.** Mince the onion and chop the mushrooms. Melt the butter in a large skillet over medium-high heat. Add the onion, mushrooms, and parsley and sauté until the onions are tender. Meanwhile, coarsely chop the anchovies and shrimp. Mix the anchovies (if using), shrimp, and breadcrumbs into the skillet. Cook for 2 additional minutes then remove the skillet from heat.

3. Place the salmon fillets in a lightly buttered baking dish. Top each fillet with 2 pieces of bacon and spoon an equal portion of the Stuffing over top. Add white wine to the baking dish.

4. Bake uncovered for 30 minutes, basting every 10 minutes with the white wine. The fish is done when it flakes easily with a fork.

Both salmon and shrimp are an excellent source of omega-3 fatty acids.

This sauce has a rich flavor from the blend of fresh and dried herbs.

Salmon Fillets in Creamy Herb Sauce

Salmon and dill are made for each other, which is why the pairing is so popular across the globe. It's best with fresh dill. The creamy herb sauce is simple to make and pairs perfectly with the fish.

Makes: 4 servings

Prep Time: 5 to 10 minutes

Cook Time: 30 to 40 minutes

Ingredients

- » 1 ½ cups mayonnaise
- » ½ cup yellow mustard
- » 1 teaspoon chopped fresh thyme
- » 1 teaspoon dried oregano
- » 1 teaspoon chopped fresh basil
- » Four ½-pound salmon fillets
- » 3 teaspoons minced fresh dill

Preparation

1. Preheat the oven to 375°F. In a medium bowl, combine the mayonnaise and mustard. Stir in the thyme, oregano, and basil and mix well. Refrigerate half of the mayonnaise mixture until ready to serve; set the other half aside.

2. Place the salmon fillets, skin side down, on a lightly greased baking sheet. Spread a generous amount of the remaining mayonnaise mixture over the fillets. Sprinkle the dill over the fillets and bake for 20 to 25 minutes or until the salmon flakes easily with a fork. Serve the fillets with the reserved mayonnaise mixture on the side.

Alaskan Salmon Chowder

Leftover cooked salmon works great in this easy-to-make preparation. Zucchini and cream-style corn, in addition to all the other vegetables, make the chowder a healthy, hearty meal during the summer.

Ingredients

- » 1 small onion
- » 2 to 3 celery stalks
- » ½ small green bell pepper
- » 1 clove garlic
- » One 14½-ounce can chicken broth, divided
- » 2 to 3 potatoes
- » 2 large carrots
- » 1 teaspoon seasoned salt
- » ½ teaspoon dried dill
- » 1 small zucchini
- » One 14¾-ounce can cream-style corn
- » One 12-ounce can evaporated milk
- » 2 cups cooked, flaked salmon

Makes: 4 to 6 servings
Prep Time: 10 minutes
Cook Time: 30 minutes

Preparation

1. Chop the onion, celery, and green pepper and mince the garlic, then place the chopped vegetables in a large saucepan or pot over medium-high heat. Add ¼ cup of the chicken broth and cook until the vegetables are tender.

2. Meanwhile, clean, peel, and dice the potatoes. Slice the carrots. Once the onions in the pot are tender, stir in the potatoes, carrots, seasoned salt, dill, and remaining chicken broth. Cover the saucepan and let the mixture simmer for 20 minutes or until all the vegetables are tender.

3. Thinly slice the zucchini and add it to the saucepan. Simmer for an additional 5 minutes. Slowly stir in the cream-style corn, evaporated milk, and salmon. Cook for 1 to 2 additional minutes or until all the ingredients are heated through.

4. To serve, ladle the salmon chowder into bowls and serve with oyster crackers or slices of crusty bread on the side.

This delicious chowder is a great way to use salmon leftovers.

Trout & Salmon **59**

Salmon & Shrimp over Garlic Rice

Best served back at the cabin after a long day on the water, salmon and shrimp go great together on garlic rice and topped with a creamy sauce. Enjoy; you earned it.

Makes: 4 to 6 servings

Prep Time: 20 minutes

Cook Time:
    25 to 30 minutes

Ingredients

- » ½ pound medium shrimp
- » 5 tablespoons butter, divided
- » 3 tablespoons flour
- » 1½ cups half-and-half
- » 1 cup shredded cheddar cheese
- » 1 teaspoon salt
- » ½ teaspoon ground mustard
- » 2 teaspoons minced fresh Italian parsley
- » Pinch cayenne pepper
- » Four to six ½-pound salmon fillets
- » 3 garlic cloves
- » 1 cup uncooked long grain rice
- » 2 cups chicken broth

Preparation

1. Preheat the oven to 400°F. Peel and devein the shrimp. Place 3 tablespoons of butter in a large saucepan over medium heat. Once the butter is melted, stir in the flour until the mixture smooth. Gradually stir in the half-and-half and mix well. Bring the mixture to a boil for 2 minutes, stirring constantly, or until the sauce is thickened. Stir in the salt, ground mustard, fresh parsley, and cayenne pepper. Remove the saucepan from heat and stir in the shrimp.

2. Rinse the salmon fillets and pat dry with paper towels. Lightly grease a 9 x 13–inch baking dish. Place the salmon fillets in the baking dish, skin side down. Pour the shrimp and sauce mixture over the salmon. Bake for 25 to 30 minutes or until the salmon flakes easily with a fork.

3. Meanwhile, mince the garlic. Place the remaining 2 tablespoons of butter in a medium saucepan over medium-high heat. Once the butter is melted, stir in the garlic and sauté until it is tender and fragrant. Add the rice and sauté, stirring often, for 2 minutes. Add the chicken broth and bring the mixture to a boil. Reduce the heat to medium-low, cover, and cook for 15 minutes or until the rice is tender.

4. To serve, place a bed of rice on each serving plate. Remove the baking dish from the oven and place a serving of salmon and shrimp with sauce over the rice.

Garlic rice is the perfect base for this salmon-based entrée.

Trout in Orange Sauce

If you are headed to the trout stream, make a batch of the Orange Sauce at home in advance, and add it to the cooked trout in camp. If desired, you can remove the spine and bones from the cooked trout by pulling up on it from the head and working your way down toward the tail. Pack an orange to serve, as a punch of citrus always improves a trout dish.

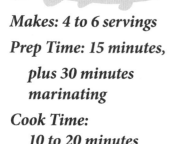

Makes: 4 to 6 servings

Prep Time: 15 minutes,
   plus 30 minutes
   marinating

Cook Time:
   10 to 20 minutes

Ingredients

Orange Sauce

» 2 green onions
» ½ cup orange juice
» 1 tablespoon lime juice
» 1 tablespoon vegetable oil
» ¼ teaspoon ground ginger
» ⅛ teaspoon salt

Trout

» Four 1-pound whole trout,
   cleaned and dressed
» ½ cup flour
» ¼ teaspoon salt
» ⅛ teaspoon pepper
» 2 tablespoons vegetable oil
» 1 orange, to serve

Preparation

1. Place the trout in a 9 x 13–inch glass baking dish.

2. **Prepare the Orange Sauce.** Slice the green onions diagonally. In a small bowl, combine the green onions, orange juice, lime juice, 1 tablespoon of vegetable oil, ground ginger, and salt and mix well. Pour the Orange Sauce over the trout. Cover and place the baking dish in the refrigerator for 30 minutes to marinate. Meanwhile, in a shallow pie plate, combine the flour, salt, and pepper and mix until well blended.

3. Remove the trout from the refrigerator and pour the Orange Sauce into a separate bowl and set it aside. Dip the trout steaks in the seasoned flour, turning to coat both sides. Meanwhile, heat the vegetable oil in a large skillet over medium-high heat.

4. Once the oil is hot, cook the fish for 10 minutes per inch of thickness, measured at the thickest part of the steaks. Turn the trout halfway through the cooking time. The fish is done when it flakes easily with a fork. Remove the trout and set it aside, keeping it warm in the oven.

5. Pour the reserved Orange Sauce into the same skillet over medium-high heat. Cook, stirring often, until the sauce is reduced to about ⅓ cup. Pour the sauce over the trout. Cut the orange into round slices and place the slices around the trout on the serving dish.

Lime juice helps boost the flavors of the citrusy sauce. Try adding orange zest to your sauce, as well, for an extra punch.

Freshwater Gamefish

Fish like striped bass make great elevated meals.

How to Process Harvested Fish Like a Pro

How harvested fish are handled once they are out of the water determines how they good they will be on the dinner plate. Many years ago, it was commonplace to leave a stringer fish hanging off the side of the boat, soaking in 90-degree water. Imagine if you found out that the trout you bought at the market was handled the same way: you would be—and should be—horrified. Instead of that outdated practice, make sure that your fish are gutted, bled (for larger fish), and put on ice as soon as possible after they are caught. Note that they need to be kept on ice, not in ice water. If you find your fish floating around the cooler in coldish water, drain the cooler and add new ice.

Once you get home, pat the fish dry and process them immediately. For the tightest seal for your frozen fish, first place them in a single layer on a lightly oiled sheet pan. Once frozen, they can be vacuum sealed, and air pockets or fishy liquids won't compromise the seal. When you are ready to start cooking, place the vacuum-sealed package under cold running water until thawed. Here is the really important part—make sure that your fish is dry before starting any recipe.

Prepare Fish for the Skillet the Right Way

Previously frozen fish will exude fishy liquids once thawed. The liquids weren't there when the fish was frozen, but it is there now. Wrap the fish in two-ply paper towels and gently give it a squeeze to wick out any liquids. If the paper towels get wet, rewrap the fish with new paper towels and continue to dry. When you add your fish to the skillet with a splash of white wine, the wine won't compete with the off-tasting fish juices and the cooked fish will taste much better, not "fishy." Keeping fish wrapped in paper towels in the refrigerator is better than storing them in a plastic bag or container. The fish will also last longer in the refrigerator as long as you replace any moist paper towels with dry ones.

Professional fish cooks know when the fish is properly cooked. If it has been handled properly, you don't need to kill it twice by overcooking. Cooking fish until it is just done, and not overcooked, will result in a more moist and flavorful meal. Best of all, if your fish is a little undercooked, you can always cook it more.

Adding a big squeeze of lemon over the cooked fish balances the sweetness of the chutney with a bit of sour.

Grilled Walleye with Fruit Chutney

It's important not to bury one of America's best-tasting freshwater fish in a mound of chutney. Just a spoonful will do. If desired, serve with additional chutney on the side.

Ingredients

Fruit Chutney

» 3 cups firm fruit, peeled, seeded, and diced into 1- to 2-inch pieces
» 1 jalapeño, seeded and minced
» ¾ cup sugar
» ½ cup white vinegar
» 2 teaspoons peeled and minced fresh ginger

Fish Fillets

» Four ½-pound walleye fillets
» 2 garlic cloves, minced
» 2 tablespoons olive oil
» Salt and pepper, to taste
» 1 lemon, quartered

Makes: 4 servings

Prep Time: 15 minutes, plus 15 minutes marinating

Cook Time: 15 minutes

Preparation

1. **Prepare the Fruit Chutney:** Combine all the ingredients in a saucepan over low heat and simmer for 1 hour or until the fruit is soft. Let the chutney rest at room temperature for 30 minutes.

2. **Prepare the Fish Fillets:** Place the walleye fillets in a large bowl. Sprinkle the garlic and olive oil over the fillets. Cover the bowl with plastic wrap and place it in the refrigerator for 1 hour to marinate.

3. Preheat an outdoor grill to medium-high heat and lightly oil the grate. Tear one piece of aluminum foil large enough to wrap around the fish fillets. Remove the fillets from the refrigerator and discard any remaining garlic or oil from the bowl. Sprinkle the fish with salt and pepper. Place the fish on the aluminum foil and wrap the foil up and over the fish, pinching the sides to enclose the fish. Place the wrapped packet on the grill over indirect heat. Grill for about 15 minutes or until the fish flakes easily with a fork.

4. To serve, remove the fish from the grill and carefully unwrap the packet. Transfer each grilled fillet to a dish. Squeeze a lemon wedge over each fish. Garnish each serving with a generous amount of the fruit chutney.

Catfish Parmesan

With the best-quality Parmesan cheese you can find, you'll do right by your fresh catfish catch, and your guests. Almond slices and breading provide the crunch, and a squeeze of fresh lime or lemon provides the high notes to the flavor of the finished dish.

Ingredients

- » ½ cup freshly grated Parmesan cheese
- » ¼ cup flour
- » ½ teaspoon salt
- » ¼ teaspoon pepper
- » 1 teaspoon paprika
- » 1 egg, beaten

- » ¼ cup milk
- » Four 6- to 8-ounce catfish fillets, skin removed
- » ¼ cup butter, melted
- » ⅓ cup almonds slices

Makes: 4 servings
Prep Time: 10 minutes
Cook Time: 40 minutes

Preparation

1. Preheat the oven to 350°F. Lightly grease a 9 x 13–inch baking dish. In a medium bowl, combine the Parmesan cheese, flour, salt, pepper, and paprika and mix until well combined. In a separate bowl, combine the beaten egg and milk.

2. Dip each catfish fillet first into the egg mixture and then into the flour mixture, turning to coat both sides. Arrange the coated catfish in the prepared baking dish.

3. Drizzle the melted butter over the catfish and sprinkle with the almonds. Bake for 20 to 25 minutes or until the fish flakes easily with a fork.

4. To serve, place each catfish fillet on a serving plate. Spoon the remaining butter and almonds from the baking dish over each serving.

This dish works well with catfish, but any other medium-firm fish is a good substitute.

Grilled Striped Bass with Fresh Tomato Salsa

This dish is best prepared in the summer when homegrown tomatoes are at their peak and you want to keep the kitchen cool and the grill hot. Many people prefer a striped bass in the five-pound range over larger. This recipe is also great wrapped in a large, warm flour tortilla but in any case, a salsa full of garden-fresh vegetables gives the bass its best showing.

Makes: 4 servings

Prep Time: 25 minutes, plus 1 hour marinating

Cook Time: 15 minutes

Ingredients

Marinade

» 1 teaspoon cracked peppercorns
» ¼ cup freshly squeezed lime juice
» 1 cup chopped fresh cilantro leaves
» ¼ cup olive oil

Fish Fillets

» Two 6- to 8-ounce striped bass fillets
» Salt and pepper, to taste

Fresh Tomato Salsa

» ½ pound Roma tomatoes, seeded and diced
» 1 jalapeño, stemmed, seeded, and finely diced
» ⅓ cup diced bell pepper
» ⅓ cup finely diced yellow onion
» ¼ cup chopped cilantro leaves
» 1 to 2 pinches ground cumin
» 4 to 6 garlic cloves, minced
» ¼ cup olive oil
» 1 avocado, peeled, seeded, and chopped
» Salt and pepper, to taste

For Serving

» Rice, cooked, to serve (optional)
» Vegetables, grilled, to serve (optional)

Preparation

1. **Prepare the Marinade.** In a medium bowl, combine the peppercorns, lime juice, cilantro, and olive oil and whisk until well combined.

2. **Prepare the Fish Fillets.** Season the fish fillets with salt and pepper. Place the fillets in a 9 x 13–inch glass or ceramic baking dish. Pour the marinade over the fillets. Cover and place the dish in the refrigerator for 1 hour.

3. Heat up the grill. Remove the fish from the refrigerator and remove the fillets from the marinade. Pat the fillets dry with paper towels and discard the marinade. Place the fish on a well-oiled, hot grill for about 3 to 4 minutes per side or until lightly browned and just cooked.

4. **Prepare the Salsa.** Combine the tomatoes, jalapeño, bell pepper, onion, cilantro, cumin, and garlic in a medium bowl. Toss the mixture, then fold in the avocado, a pinch salt, and a pinch of pepper.

5. To serve, place the grilled fish on warm rice or grilled vegetables. Top each fillet with a spoonful of salsa.

Tomatoes complement the flavors of the grilled bass.

Fresh greens always work well as a side for baked fillets.

Breaded Baked Walleye

When it comes to cooking walleye, keep it simple to preserve the delicious, moist, and flaky fillets. And this dish is simple: marinate, bake, and go.

Ingredients

- » One 2-pound walleye fillet
- » 1 cup milk
- » ½ cup breadcrumbs
- » ½ teaspoon salt
- » ½ teaspoon pepper
- » 1 tablespoon chopped fresh parsley
- » 1 green onion
- » ½ cup butter, melted
- » 1 lemon

Makes: 4 to 6 servings

Prep Time: 10 minutes, plus 30 minutes soaking

Cook Time: 25 minutes

Preparation

1. Cut the walleye fillets into 4 to 6 pieces, depending on how many servings you prefer. Place the fish pieces in a medium bowl and pour the milk over top. Cover the bowl and place it in the refrigerator for 30 minutes to soak.

2. Preheat the oven to 350°F. Grease a 9 x 13–inch glass baking dish and set aside. In a shallow pie plate, combine the breadcrumbs, salt, pepper, and parsley. Remove the walleye from the refrigerator and discard the milk. Roll the fish pieces in the breadcrumb mixture until they are evenly coated. Place the coated fish pieces in the greased baking dish.

3. Chop the green onion and sprinkle it over the fish in the baking dish. Drizzle the melted butter over the fish. Bake, uncovered, for 20 minutes or until the fish flakes easily with a fork. To serve, cut the lemon into wedges. Place one fish piece on each serving plate and garnish with a wedge of lemon.

Parmesan-Baked Pike in Tomato Sauce

The challenge with any of the pike species is getting a clean fillet with the Y bones removed. It takes some practice, but once processed the fillets are delicious. Unlike many other species, pike skin is best removed for the best flavor when cooked.

Ingredients

» One 1 ½-pound pike fillet
» ⅓ cup olive oil
» 2 tablespoons lemon juice
» ½ cup fine breadcrumbs
» ½ cup grated Parmesan cheese, plus more for topping
» 1 tablespoon chopped fresh parsley
» Salt and pepper, to taste
» 1 medium tomato
» 1 tablespoon chopped or whole capers
» 1 tablespoon chopped fresh basil
» 2 tablespoons dry white wine
» 1 tablespoon butter

Makes: 4 servings
Prep Time: 10 minutes
Cook Time: 12 to 15 minutes

Preparation

1. Preheat the oven to 500°F. Lightly grease a baking sheet. Cut the fillet into 4 pieces.

2. Combine the olive oil and lemon juice in a medium bowl. In a shallow pie plate, combine the breadcrumbs, Parmesan cheese, parsley, salt, and pepper and mix well. Dip the fillets into the olive oil mixture and then into the breadcrumb mixture, turning to coat both sides. Place the coated fish pieces on the prepared baking sheet. Bake for 12 to 15 minutes.

3. Meanwhile, chop the tomato. Place the tomato in a medium saucepan over medium-high heat. Add the capers and basil and sauté for 1 to 2 minutes. Slowly pour in the white wine. Bring the mixture to a boil and add the butter in small pieces, stirring just until the butter melts. Remove the saucepan from heat and season the sauce with salt and pepper to taste.

4. To serve, transfer each baked fish piece to a serving plate. Drizzle a generous amount of the tomato sauce mixture over each serving. Top each serving with a sprinkling of additional Parmesan cheese.

Homemade tomato sauce will elevate almost any savory dish and this one is no exception.

Spinach & Crappie Casserole

Although less common in many parts of the country than in decades past, casseroles are still a big deal, especially when the weather runs cold and a single-pan dish with all the nutrients you need smells and tastes best. If you're in the mood for comfort food, look no further. This recipe also works well with semi-firm panfish like bluegill or sauger.

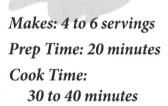

Makes: 4 to 6 servings
Prep Time: 20 minutes
Cook Time:
   30 to 40 minutes

Ingredients
- » 3 celery stalks
- » 1 small onion
- » 2 garlic cloves
- » 2 tablespoons olive oil
- » 4 tablespoons butter, divided
- » 1 ½ cups chopped fresh spinach
- » 2 cups mushrooms, sliced
- » 1 ½ pounds crappie pieces
- » 1 cup soft breadcrumbs, divided
- » 2 eggs, beaten
- » Salt and pepper, to taste
- » Pinch dried dill
- » ⅓ cup crumbled feta cheese
- » Pinch paprika
- » Dash lemon juice

Preparation

1. Chop the celery and onion and mince the garlic. Place the olive oil and 1 tablespoon of butter in a large skillet over medium-high heat. Add the celery, onion, and garlic and sauté until the vegetables are tender. Add the spinach and continue to cook, stirring, until the spinach wilts. Add the mushrooms to the skillet and cook, stirring until heated through. Set the skillet aside and cover it to keep the vegetables warm.

2. Lightly grease a 9-inch-square glass baking dish. Place half of the fish pieces in one layer across the bottom. Spread half of the breadcrumbs over the fish and pour the beaten eggs over the breadcrumbs. Sprinkle with salt, pepper, and dill. Next, spread the sautéed vegetables over the ingredients in the baking dish and press down lightly.

3. Sprinkle the feta cheese over the vegetables. Create a second layer with the remaining fish pieces. Season with salt, pepper, and a pinch of paprika. Sprinkle the remaining breadcrumbs on top. Pour 3 tablespoons of butter, melted, over the casserole and top with a dash of lemon juice. Cover the baking dish with aluminum foil. Bake for 30 minutes or until the fish is opaque.

4. To serve, remove the baking dish from the oven and cut the casserole into squares.

If crappie is not available, other semifirm panfish will work well.

Fish Fingers in Ragout Sauce

This preparation combines fresh fish fillets with a buttery mushroom sauce and a hint of white wine as well as a healthy herbal jolt of parsley. Feel free to substitute or add other fresh vegetables or herbs to the dish.

Ingredients

» 3 pounds fish fillets, skin removed
» 1 cup flour
» 1 teaspoon salt
» ½ teaspoon pepper
» 1 tablespoon butter, plus 1 teaspoon
» 1 tablespoon olive oil, plus 1 teaspoon
» ½ cup thinly sliced mushrooms

» 2 tablespoons finely chopped black olives
» 1 can artichoke bottoms (or hearts), quartered
» ⅓ cup dry white wine
» 3 tablespoons chopped fresh parsley
» 1 tablespoon lemon juice
» 3 tomatoes, seeded and diced

Makes: 6 to 8 servings

Prep Time: 25 minutes

Cook Time: 10 minutes

Preparation

1. Cut the fish into 3-to-4-inch strips. In a small bowl, combine the flour, salt, and pepper and mix well. Dust each fish strip with the seasoned flour on all sides.

2. Heat 1 tablespoon of butter and 1 tablespoon of olive oil in a large skillet over medium-high heat. Place the coated fish strips in the skillet and cook until they are golden brown, turning to cook both sides. Remove the fish from the skillet and keep them warm.

3. Add 1 teaspoon of butter and 1 teaspoon of olive oil into the same skillet over medium heat. Stir in the mushrooms, black olives, artichoke bottoms, wine, parsley, and lemon juice. Cook, stirring, for 2 to 3 minutes. Mix in the tomatoes and cook for 1 minute. Return the warm fish strips to the skillet and turn until they are coated in the sauce. Transfer the cooked fish to plates or a serving platter and top with the sauce from the pan.

Walleye, Capers & Lemon

Don't ruin your recipe with unpalatable cooking wine from the grocery store. Any inexpensive, unflavored, neutral wine like a Chablis works great. Of course, if you buy a better wine that you can enjoy with the recipe, you'll only need a splash for the cooking part. You can either leave the skin on the fillets or take it off. Capers, lemon juice, and green onions always bring out the best in fish.

Potatoes are a great side for this dish.

Ingredients

- » Four 6- to 8-ounce walleye fillets
- » ½ cup all-purpose flour
- » 1 teaspoon salt
- » ¼ teaspoon white pepper
- » ½ teaspoon garlic powder
- » 1 to 2 pinches Italian seasoning
- » 5 tablespoons butter, divided
- » 3 tablespoons olive oil
- » 2 tablespoons freshly squeezed lemon juice
- » ¼ cup dry white wine
- » Pinch sugar
- » 1 tablespoon capers
- » 2 green onions, chopped
- » ½ cup seeded and diced tomato

Makes: 4 servings
Prep Time: 10 minutes
Cook Time: 10 to 12 minutes

Preparation

1. Pat the fillets dry with paper towels. Combine the flour with the salt, white pepper, garlic powder, and Italian seasoning. Dust the fish with the seasoned flour. Heat 2 tablespoons of the butter and the olive oil in a large skillet over medium heat. Add the fish (skin side down, if intact) and brown them lightly on both sides until just cooked. Transfer the fish to a dish or pan, cover, and keep warm in a 200°F oven.

2. Wipe out the pan with a paper towel and return the pan to the stove over medium heat. Add the lemon juice, wine, sugar, and capers. Bring the mixture to a boil and reduce the liquid to 1 or 2 tablespoons. Remove the pan from heat and whisk in the remaining 3 tablespoons of butter and the green onions until the butter is melted. Stir in the tomato and spoon the sauce over the warm fish to serve.

Next-Day Fish Cakes

What to do with leftover cooked fish? Don't let it take up residence in the refrigerator; bring it out for this recipe, which converts leftover cooked fish into cakes that taste remarkably—and deliciously—like crab cakes. For best results, make this recipe a day or two after your fish is cooked.

Makes: 4 servings
Prep Time: 25 minutes
Cook Time: 4 minutes

Ingredients

- » 1 pound cooked fish fillets
- » 2 tablespoons flour, plus more as needed
- » 1 medium onion, minced
- » 1 teaspoon yellow mustard
- » 1 tablespoon mayonnaise, plus more as needed
- » ½ teaspoon Old Bay seasoning
- » 2½ cups panko, plus more as needed
- » 1 egg
- » ½ cup vegetable oil
- » Tartar sauce or cocktail sauce, to serve

Preparation

1. Wrap the cooked fish fillets in paper towels and press firmly to remove excess moisture. Using a fork, shred the fish. Sprinkle the flour evenly over the fish while tossing to mix well. Add the onion, yellow mustard, mayo, Old Bay, panko, and egg and mix well.

2. Take a portion of the mixture and form it into a ball about the size of a golf ball and press firmly. If it holds together, return it to the rest of the fish cake mixture. If it falls apart, add a little more mayonnaise. It should be a little moist, like cookie dough. If it's too moist, add more flour or breadcrumbs.

3. Heat the vegetable oil over medium heat in a large skillet. Meanwhile, form the fish cake mixture into 6 to 8 patties of even thickness. Once the oil is hot, fry the patties in the skillet for 2 to 4 minutes on each side or until lightly browned. Remove the patties and set them aside on paper towels to drain.

4. Serve hot with tartar sauce or cocktail sauce on the side.

It's always a perk to use leftovers in a delightful meal.

Sautéed Panfish with Lemon-Dill Butter

This preparation brings out the flavor of any panfish fillets. Lightly dusting the fillets in seasoned flour enhances browning and adds a tasty crust to the cooked fish. You can prepare the fish with the skin on or off, to your preference.

Makes: 4 servings

Prep Time: 25 minutes, plus 1 hour marinating

Cook Time: 15 minutes

Ingredients

- » 1 lemon, plus 1 for garnish
- » ⅓ cup butter, softened
- » 1 tablespoon finely chopped green onion
- » ½ teaspoon dried dill
- » ⅛ teaspoon white pepper
- » Four 6- to 8-ounce panfish fillets
- » 2 tablespoons flour
- » ¼ teaspoon paprika
- » ½ teaspoon salt, plus more to taste
- » ¼ teaspoon pepper, plus more to taste
- » 1 tablespoon olive oil

Preparation

1. Using a zester or vegetable peeler, remove the rind of 1 lemon and mince the peel, setting aside the fruit of the lemon. Place the minced lemon zest in a small bowl and then add the butter, green onion, dill, and white pepper. Squeeze the juice of the zested lemon into the butter mixture and stir to blend.

2. Lightly pat the fish fillets dry with paper towels. In a shallow plate or bowl, combine the flour, paprika, salt, and pepper. Dip each fish piece in the flour mixture, turning until it is lightly coated on both sides. Heat the olive oil in a large skillet over medium-high heat

3. Sauté the fish for 3 to 4 minutes per side or until evenly browned. Remove the fish from the skillet and set them aside on dry paper towels to drain. Season the fish with salt and pepper on both sides.

4. To serve, place each fillet on a serving plate. Cut the remaining lemon into 4 wedges and garnish each serving with 1 lemon wedge. Spread 2 to 3 teaspoons of the lemon-dill butter over each piece of fish and serve immediately.

A one-pan dish makes this an easy prep for any night of the week.

Use real, whole lemons for the freshest sauce.

Crappie with Lemon-Pepper Sauce

Homemade lemon-pepper sauce is a big improvement over the bottled stuff at the market. This is a simple one-pan recipe that can be prepared using any mild, lighter-fleshed fish but crappie is the choice here. You can prepare the fish with the skin on or off, to your preference.

Ingredients

- » 8 crappie fillets (from 4 fish)
- » Salt and pepper, to taste
- » 1 tablespoon olive oil
- » 4 tablespoons butter, divided
- » 2 tablespoons freshly squeezed lemon juice
- » 1 tablespoon freshly ground black pepper
- » 3 garlic cloves, minced

Makes: 4 servings

Prep Time: 15 minutes, plus 30 minutes marinating

Cook Time: 6 to 10 minutes

Preparation

1. Season the crappie fillets with salt and pepper. Heat the olive oil and 1 tablespoon of the butter in a large skillet over medium-high heat. Add the fish and lightly brown them on both sides, about 3 to 4 minutes per side. Remove the fish and keep them warm in the oven.

2. Reduce the heat to low. Add the remaining 3 tablespoons of butter, the lemon juice, freshly ground black pepper, and garlic to the skillet. Add a pinch of salt. Be careful not to overheat the sauce or it will break. Once the sauce is emulsified, place the cooked fish on plates and top each fillet with the pan sauce.

Pan-Fried Bluegill

Bluegill and other small panfish are the perfect target for new anglers. They are easy to catch, plentiful, and taste great.

Makes: 4 servings
Prep Time: 10 to 15 minutes
Cook Time: 6 to 10 minutes

Ingredients

» 1 egg
» 6 ounces light beer
» 4 bluegill fillets
» 1 to 2 cups cracker meal or crushed saltine crackers
» 2 tablespoons butter

» 2 tablespoons vegetable oil
» 2 lemons, to serve
» 12 cherry tomatoes, to serve
» 4 green onions, to serve
» 2 tablespoons capers, drained, to serve

Preparation

1. In a medium bowl, combine the egg and beer and whisk together until well blended.

2. Rinse the fillets and pat them dry with paper towels. Spread the cracker meal in a shallow pie plate. Dip each bluegill fillet into the egg mixture, letting the excess drip off. Next, dredge each fillet in the cracker meal until it is evenly coated on both sides.

It doesn't take long to pan-fry these fillets.

3. Place the butter and vegetable oil in a large skillet over medium-high heat. Once the butter is melted and the oil is very hot, place the coated fillets in the skillet and cook for 3 to 5 minutes. Turn the fillets over and cook for an additional 3 to 5 minutes or until they are nicely browned on both sides.

4. Cut the lemons in half. Quarter the cherry tomatoes and chop the green onions. To serve, place one bluegill fillet on each serving plate. Serve each with 1 lemon half, some cherry tomatoes, some green onions, and a few capers.

Southern-Style Pan-Fried Catfish

Depending on where you grew up, there's a chance that you've never had the pleasure of dining on properly prepared catfish. For the best flavor when cooked, it's important to remove as much of the "bloodline" or "mud line" that runs down the skin side of each fillet before cooking. You can use any type of cornmeal—white, yellow, or blue.

Makes: 8 servings

Prep Time: 15 minutes, plus 35 minutes soaking

Cook Time: 6 to 10 minutes

Ingredients

» 3 to 4 pounds catfish fillets, skin removed
» Salt, as needed
» ½ cup flour
» ½ cup cornmeal
» ¼ cup finely minced green onions
» ½ teaspoon sea salt
» ½ teaspoon cayenne pepper
» 1 tablespoon minced fresh parsley, divided
» 1 cup milk
» 1 cup butter
» 1 lemon, cut into wedges, for garnish
» 6 sprigs fresh parsley, for garnish

Preparation

1. Cut the catfish fillets into chunks or to your preferred serving size. Rinse the fillets in cold water, pat them dry, then soak the pieces in a bowl of lightly salted water for 30 minutes.

2. Combine the flour, cornmeal, green onions, sea salt, and cayenne pepper in a shallow pie plate and toss until well combined. Cut the lemon into 6 wedges and dust the center edge of each wedge with a little minced parsley; set aside. Add the remaining parsley to the flour mixture.

3. Drain and rinse the fish. Pour the milk into a medium bowl and then place the fish pieces in the milk and allow them to soak for 5 minutes.

4. Dip each piece of fish in the flour mixture, pressing lightly and turning to coat both sides. Place the butter in a large skillet over medium-high heat and melt the butter.

5. Add the coated fish pieces and cook for 3 to 5 minutes per side or until the coating is golden. Remove the fried fish pieces from the skillet and place them on paper towels to drain.

6. To serve, place the fish pieces on serving dishes and garnish with the lemon wedges and fresh parsley sprigs.

Preparation of this dish
before cooking is key
to achieving just the
right texture.

Use freshly grated cheddar rather than pre-shredded if you have the option.

Cheese-Stuffed Pike Corn Cakes

Sweetcorn, milk, egg, biscuit mix, and cornmeal give this cake batter a real savory thickness, and a bit of sweetness, that pairs well with the fish and Cajun spice used in the filling. Using freshly grated cheddar is ideal if you have the option over pre-shredded. The corn can be fresh or frozen.

Makes: 6 to 8 servings

Prep Time: 20 minutes

Cook Time: 10 to 15 minutes

Ingredients

Batter
- » 1 ½ cups biscuit baking mix
- » 1 egg
- » 1 ⅓ cups milk
- » 2 cups sweet corn
- » ½ cup seasoned cornmeal breading mix

Filling
- » One 8-ounce package cream cheese, softened
- » ½ teaspoon Cajun seasoning
- » 1 cup finely shredded sharp cheddar cheese
- » 1 teaspoon dried basil

Fillets
- » One 2- to 2½-pound pike fillet
- » 1 to 2 tablespoons vegetable oil

Preparation

1. **Prepare the Batter.** In a blender or food processor, combine the biscuit baking mix, egg, milk, corn, and cornmeal breading mix. Process on high until the ingredients are well combined but the corn is still lumpy. Transfer the batter to a medium bowl.

2. **Prepare the Filling.** In a separate bowl, combine the cream cheese, Cajun seasoning, cheddar cheese, and basil. Mix until well combined.

3. Cut the pike fillet into serving-size pieces about ¾ inch thick. Use a sharp, thin knife to split each piece in half again, being careful not to cut all the way through. Fold each fish piece open like a book. Place a few spoonfuls of the cream cheese mixture on one side of each fillet and fold the fish back over the filling.

4. Place a large, deep skillet over medium-high heat and add the vegetable oil. Once the oil is hot, place a generous spoonful of the batter in the pan. Set one of the filled fish pieces over the batter and spoon more batter over the fish. Heat until the batter begins to brown. Gently and quickly turn the fish over and heat until the batter is golden brown. Cut a small slit in one side of the coating to make sure the fish is opaque and cooked through. Repeat with the remaining batter and fish pieces.

Panfish Stir-Fry

Make sure that all of your ingredients are prepped and ready to add to the wok or skillet ahead of time because being quick at the wok is essential. Try this with firm to semi-firm fish fillets, but be careful when adding the fish so that it doesn't break apart when cooking.

Ingredients

- » 2 to 3 celery stalks
- » 1 green bell pepper
- » 3 green onions
- » 4 to 6 panfish fillets
- » 2 tablespoons vegetable oil
- » 1 tablespoon cornstarch
- » 3 garlic cloves, minced
- » 1 teaspoon peeled and minced fresh ginger
- » ¼ cup soy sauce
- » 1 ½ cups chicken broth or fish stock
- » Rice or noodles, cooked, to serve

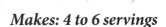

Makes: 4 to 6 servings

Prep Time: 10 to 15 minutes

Cook Time: 6 to 10 minutes

Preparation

1. Cut the celery stalks diagonally into ¼-inch slices. Cut the green pepper into ¼-inch strips. Chop the green onions. Set aside the chopped vegetables. Cut the fish fillets into 1½-inch strips. Place the vegetable oil in a large, heavy skillet or wok over medium-high heat.

2. Stir-fry the crappie strips until they are golden brown. Transfer the cooked fish to a plate and keep them warm in the oven.

3. Add the celery, green pepper strips, and green onions to the skillet and cook for 3 minutes, stirring constantly.

4. In a small bowl, combine the cornstarch, garlic, ginger, soy sauce, and chicken broth. Add the cornstarch mixture to the skillet. Bring the mixture to a boil for 3 minutes or until the sauce is thickened and hot. Return the cooked fish to the skillet and heat to serving temperature.

5. To serve, place a bed of hot, cooked rice or noodles on each serving plate and spoon some of the stir-fried fish, vegetables, and sauce over the rice.

Add snap peas to your skillet stir fry for a crunchy pop.

Fried Fish Tacos

This recipe for tacos stuffed with battered and fried fish nuggets is a clear winner. It's got flavor, texture, and just enough heat to get your attention. Use any medium-firm or firm fish fillets. Use a ripe avocado to balance out the crunch with smoothness.

Makes: 6 servings

Prep Time:
15 minutes, plus
8 hours marinating
Cook Time: 15 minutes

Ingredients

Batter

» ¾ cup flour
» ½ teaspoon baking powder
» ½ teaspoon dried oregano
» ½ teaspoon garlic powder
» ½ teaspoon chili powder
» ¼ teaspoon cayenne pepper
» Pinch salt
» Pinch pepper
» 1 egg yolk
» 4 to 6 ounces beer

Sauce

» ½ cup mayonnaise
» 1 tablespoon chopped fresh cilantro
» Juice of ½ lime

Fillets

» 1 to 1½ pounds fish fillets
» Six 6-inch corn or flour tortillas
» 1 avocado
» 2 cups shredded lettuce
» 1 lime, cut into 6 wedges
» Oil, as needed, for frying

Preparation

1. In a medium bowl, combine the flour, baking powder, oregano, garlic powder, chili powder, cayenne pepper, salt, pepper, egg yolk, and beer and mix until well combined. Cover the bowl with plastic wrap and place it in the refrigerator for 8 hours or overnight.

2. In a large, deep skillet, add oil to a depth of 2 inches and heat the oil to 375°F. In a small bowl, combine the mayonnaise, cilantro, and lime juice. Chop the fish into bite-size pieces. Remove the batter from the refrigerator and drop the fish pieces into the batter. They should be well coated.

3. Gently drop 1 or 2 pieces of battered fish at a time in the hot oil and fry for 3 to 5 minutes, turning the pieces after 2 minutes. Remove the fried fish pieces and set them aside on paper towels to drain. Repeat with the remaining fish and batter.

4. Meanwhile, wrap the flour tortillas in damp paper towels. Microwave the wrapped tortillas for 1 minute or until they are soft and pliable. Cut the avocado into slices.

5. To assemble a taco, place a few pieces of fried fish in a tortilla. Top with a few slices of avocado, a little shredded lettuce, and a drizzling of the mayonnaise sauce. Repeat with the remaining ingredients. Squeeze a little fresh lime juice over each taco before folding.

Everyone loves tacos, and everyone loves fried fish nuggets. What's better than the two together?

Crispy Catfish with Lemon-Lime Tartar Sauce

The masa harina gives a wonderful, tasty texture to chopped catfish. It's the processed corn flour used to make tamales. It's probably in your market, but you may not know it's there. Look for a bag in the Hispanic or baking sections of your store. You can use regular Tabasco or Chipotle Tabasco sauce for a smoky kick.

Ingredients

Batter

» 3 eggs, beaten
» 2 tablespoons yellow mustard
» 2 to 3 garlic cloves, minced
» 1 teaspoon salt
» ½ teaspoon black pepper
» Dash Tabasco sauce
» ⅓ cup milk

Dry Coating

» 1 cup masa harina flour
» 1 cup cornmeal
» 1 tablespoon salt
» 1 teaspoon black pepper

Lemon-Lime Tartar Sauce

» 1 cup mayonnaise
» 2 garlic cloves, minced
» 1 tablespoon sweet pickle relish
» 1 tablespoon lime juice
» 1 tablespoon yellow mustard
» 1 tablespoon minced fresh parsley
» 1 teaspoon capers, drained
» 1 teaspoon lemon zest
» 1 teaspoon lemon juice
» 1 teaspoon lime zest

Fillets

» 1 ½ pounds catfish fillets, cut into 1-inch-wide strips
» Oil, as needed, for frying

Makes: 4 servings

Prep Time: 15 to 20 minutes

Cook Time: 5 minutes

Preparation

1. **Prepare the Batter.** In a medium bowl, combine all of the ingredients. Set aside.

2. **Prepare the Dry Coating**. In a shallow bowl, combine all of the ingredients. Set aside.

3. **Prepare the Lemon-Lime Tartar Sauce.** In a small bowl, combine all of the ingredients and mix well. Refrigerate the sauce for 1 hour.

4. Heat the oil in a deep, heavy-duty pot or fryer. Dredge the fish fillets first in the batter bowl, then coat them in the Dry Coating. Using tongs, carefully place each piece, 1 or 2 at a time, into the hot oil. Fry until they are golden brown and then drain the fish on paper towels. Season the fish with additional salt and pepper as desired while they are still hot. Serve with the Lemon-Lime Tartar Sauce on the side.

Masa harina (harina flour) is the necessary ingredient to make this dish.

Cajun seasoning can range in a variety of spice levels depending on your palate.

Cajun Catfish Wraps

Just because it's Cajun doesn't mean it has to be spicy. Adjust the seasonings to fit your palate. If you like it hot, add a few splashes of your favorite hot sauce. The coleslaw adds a sweet and crunchy dimension to the wraps.

Ingredients

Coleslaw

» 2 green onions, finely chopped
» 3½ cups finely shredded cabbage
» ¼ cup mayonnaise
» 1½ tablespoons apple cider vinegar
» ½ teaspoon sugar
» 3 tablespoons chopped fresh cilantro

Seasoning

» 1 tablespoon flour
» 1 tablespoon paprika
» 1½ teaspoons dried thyme
» 1½ teaspoons dried oregano
» 1 teaspoon garlic powder
» 1 teaspoon pepper
» ½ teaspoon salt
» ¼ teaspoon cayenne pepper

Fish

» 1½ pounds catfish pieces
» 1 tablespoon butter
» 4 to 6 flour tortillas

Makes: 4 servings

Prep Time: 15 minutes

Cook Time: 10 minutes

Preparation

1. **Prepare the Coleslaw.** In a medium bowl, combine the green onions, cabbage, mayonnaise, apple cider vinegar, sugar, and cilantro. Mix everything together until the ingredients are well combined and evenly coated with mayonnaise. Chill the Coleslaw in the refrigerator until ready to serve.

2. **Prepare the Seasoning.** In a small bowl, combine the flour, paprika, thyme, oregano, garlic powder, pepper, salt, and cayenne pepper.

3. Rinse the catfish pieces and pat them dry with paper towels. Dredge the catfish pieces in the Seasoning mixture.

4. Place the butter in a large, heavy skillet over medium heat. Once the butter is melted, sauté the catfish pieces for 5 minutes. Carefully turn them over and cook for 4 minutes on the other side.

5. Wrap the flour tortillas in damp paper towels and microwave them for 30 seconds or until the tortillas are pliable. Divide the cooked catfish pieces between the tortillas. Top each serving with about ¾ cup of the Coleslaw. Fold the sides in and wrap to enclose the fish and Coleslaw.

Walleye & Kraut Sandwiches

It might seem odd to combine a mild, flaky fish like walleye with crunchy, tart sauerkraut, but you do have to give this one a try. It's like a Rueben sandwich but without the corned beef. Try it with a side of thousand island dressing dipping sauce.

Ingredients

- » 1½ cups cooked, flaked walleye
- » ½ cup sauerkraut, drained
- » ¼ cup chopped dill pickles
- » ¼ cup mayonnaise
- » ¼ cup butter, softened, plus 2 tablespoons
- » 8 slices rye bread
- » 4 slices Swiss cheese

Makes: 4 servings

Prep Time: 15 minutes

Cook Time: 12 to 16 minutes

Preparation

1. In a medium bowl, combine the walleye, sauerkraut, dill pickles, and mayonnaise and mix until well combined.

2. Spread ¼ cup of butter over one side of each rye bread slice. Divide and spread the walleye mixture evenly onto the unbuttered sides of 4 slices of bread. Top with the slices of Swiss cheese. Place the remaining bread slices on top, buttered side out.

3. Melt the remaining 2 tablespoons of butter in a medium skillet over medium heat. Once the butter is melted, place the sandwiches in the skillet and grill for 3 to 4 minutes on each side or until the bread is golden brown and the filling is heated through.

4. To serve, place each sandwich on a plate and cut diagonally into halves.

If you have the time and bandwidth, making your own homemade sauerkraut will elevate this dish to fantastic heights.

Upland Game

Quail eggs are very distinctive among bird eggs.

Depending on where you live, access to upland game will vary. South Dakota is famous for large populations of ringneck pheasants. Montana has pheasants, too, but they also have good huntable populations of sharptailed grouse and Hungarian partridges. Wild turkeys have exploded in population and can be found in every American state except Alaska. Rabbits, ever popular furred targets, are a good starter species for new hunters and a lot can be done with their meat in the kitchen or at the grill.

It All Starts with a Good Bird Dog

If you are an experienced bird hunter, you fully understand the importance of a good bird dog. Whether yours is a Labrador retriever who does not hesitate to fly out of the blind to retrieve your mallard or a setter on solid point along a hedge row, without the dogs, you might not see—or retrieve—your birds. Good bird hunters also know to carry plastic bags and a cooler with ice for the drive home. Many misguided hunters will trudge up and down hills in 60°F weather with a quail, pheasant, or chukar in their game bags. Imagine the public outcry if your local chicken processor treated your store-bought chickens with the same carelessness. Stop by the truck every hour or so to transfer game birds to a cooler. Later, when cooked, the birds will taste better.

Break Down Larger Birds

Larger upland game birds like pheasants and wild turkeys should generally be cooked in parts, not as whole birds. Sinewy legs and thighs should be cooked for a few hours with low, moist heat. The breasts cook quickly in a medium-hot skillet. If you do not have enough of any one type of game bird to make a meal, combine the parts of a variety of birds to make a hearty stew. Whatever parts are left over, like the necks and carcasses, can be roasted and submerged into a stock pot with onions, celery, and carrots to make a sensational broth. That's a responsible way of harvesting these animals that also gives you the ingredients to make a savory stock that puts salty bouillon cubes to shame.

Pluck Like a Pro

Game bird feathers can be plucked or picked. Prior to plucking, submerge the bird in 185°F to 200°F water for a few seconds, remove it from the water, and give it a good shake. Then plunge the bird into the hot water another time, shake, and start plucking. The feathers will be much easier to remove after the hot water treatment. While there is not much fat on wild bird skin, it does crisp up nicely when cooked properly.

Cut the breast across the grain for best results.

Grilled Sesame Turkey Breast

When preparing wild turkey, cut the breast meat across the grain for best results. If you want this recipe to really pay off for all the hard work of harvesting the wild turkey, you'll want to buy the best-quality sesame oil you can find to serve as the foundation for the marinade. The smell of sesame-basted turkey cooking on the grill will be a sensory experience in itself.

Makes: 4 servings

Prep Time: 10 minutes, plus
8 hours marinating

Cook Time: 15 minutes

Ingredients

Turkey
» 1 whole wild turkey breast

Sesame Marinade
» 1 cup soy sauce
» 1 cup brown sugar
» ¼ cup sesame oil
» ½ cup sesame seeds
» 2 tablespoons pepper
» 10 green onions, minced
» 10 garlic cloves, minced
» 1 tablespoon fresh grated ginger
» 2 tablespoons butter, melted

Preparation

1. Cut the turkey breast into serving-size pieces, cutting across the grain.

2. **Prepare the Sesame Marinade.** In a medium bowl, combine all of the ingredients and mix well. Set aside and refrigerate ½ to ¾ cup of the Sesame Marinade, for basting, before adding the turkey breast pieces to the bowl. Add the turkey pieces to the bowl, turning until evenly coated. Place the bowl in the refrigerator for 8 hours or overnight to marinate.

3. Preheat the grill to medium-high heat. Remove the bowl from the refrigerator and discard the marinade. Place the turkey pieces on the grill over indirect heat. Though this will take longer to cook, the meat won't dry out as easily over indirect heat. Grill the turkey pieces for about 10 to 15 minutes or until cooked through, basting often with the reserved marinade. The meat will be done when it reaches an internal temperature of 160°F as measured on a meat thermometer.

Pheasant Breast with Peach Glaze

If possible, take the time to pluck, rather than peel, your pheasants. Although lean pheasant skin doesn't add much fat to the dish, the texture of crispy skin adds just enough crunch. You can prepare the pheasant with the skin on or off, to your preference. The peach glaze gets this dish ready to headline an extra special summer picnic.

Ingredients

Pheasant Breasts
» 2 whole pheasant breasts
» ¼ cup butter, melted
» Salt and pepper, to taste
» Paprika, to taste

Peach Glaze
» One 15-ounce can peach halves in syrup
» ½ cup sugar
» 3 tablespoons brandy
» Dash cinnamon or nutmeg

Makes: 4 servings
Prep Time: 10 to 15 minutes
Cook Time: 6 to 10 minutes

Preparation

1. Preheat the oven to 350°F. Brush the pheasant breasts with the melted butter. Season both sides of each breast with salt and pepper and dust with paprika. Tightly wrap each pheasant breast separately in a sheet of aluminum foil. Place the wrapped pheasant breasts on a baking sheet and place them in the oven. Bake for 25 to 30 minutes.

2. **Prepare the Peach Glaze.** In a blender, place 4 of the canned peach halves. Add ¼ cup of the liquid syrup from the canned peaches to the blender. Reserve any remaining peach halves and syrup for future use. To the blender, add the sugar, brandy, and cinnamon or nutmeg. Place the lid on the blender and process until well blended and smooth. Pour the blended peach mixture into a medium saucepan over medium heat. Bring the Peach Glaze to a boil and remove it from heat.

Peach glaze makes any dish perfect for a summer picnic.

3. Remove the pheasant breasts from the oven and carefully open the aluminum packets. Brush a generous amount of the Peach Glaze over each pheasant breast. Keeping the aluminum packets open, return the pheasant breasts to the oven and bake for 5 more minutes.

4. To serve, drizzle the remaining glaze over the serving plates. Place one pheasant breast or pheasant breast half over the glaze on each plate.

Grilled Quail with Sweet Bacon Sauce

Bacon and wild game are an unbeatable combination. Sweet bacon sauce provides a rich, sweet complement to lean game bird meat. Haricot verts are long French green beans, for those who don't know, and they can be picked up at your local farmers market or, barring that, the grocery store.

Makes: 2 servings
Prep Time: 15 minutes,
*   plus 2 hours*
*   marinating*
Cook Time:
*   30 to 45 minutes*

Ingredients

Quail

- » 4 whole quail
- » ¼ cup olive oil
- » 1 teaspoon garlic powder
- » 1 teaspoon ground coriander

Sweet Bacon Sauce

- » 1 small onion
- » 1 clove garlic
- » 3 bacon strips
- » 1 teaspoon red wine vinegar
- » 1½ teaspoons honey
- » ½ cup haricot verts
- » 2 tablespoons minced fresh cilantro leaves
- » Salt and pepper, to taste

Preparation

1. Place the quail in a medium bowl. Pour the olive oil over top and sprinkle with the garlic powder and ground coriander, turning the quail to coat both sides. Place the bowl in the refrigerator for 2 hours to marinate.

2. **Prepare the Sweet Bacon Sauce.** Dice the onion and mince the garlic and set aside. In a medium skillet over medium-high heat, cook the bacon strips until tender. Remove the bacon and set it aside on paper towels to drain; reserve 1 teaspoon of the bacon drippings in the pan. Crumble the bacon and return it to the pan. Add the onion and garlic to the pan and sauté until the onions are translucent. Add the red wine vinegar and cook until almost all of the liquid has been absorbed. Stir in the honey and simmer for 1 additional minute. Add the haricot verts and cilantro. Season with salt and pepper to taste and reduce the heat to very low to keep the sauce warm while grilling the quail.

3. Preheat the grill to medium heat. Remove the quail from the refrigerator and discard the marinade. Grill the quail for 15 to 18 minutes or until the meat is just cooked (and not overcooked).

4. To serve, place 2 grilled quail on each serving plate. Spoon a generous amount of the haricot verts and Sweet Bacon Sauce over each serving.

Most people can easily eat two quail for a big meal, but that can change depending on the sides and toppings you serve with it.

Red Currant–Roasted Pheasant

Red currant jelly is a unique and delicious flavor that somehow goes perfectly with all kinds of wild game meat, pheasant chief among them. Reserve the leftover pheasant carcass to make a savory stock, if desired: Place the carcass in a stock pot with rough chopped onion, carrot, and celery. Cover with cold water and simmer, uncovered, for 8 to 12 hours. Add more water as needed. Pour it through a colander and use the stock for soups and sauces.

Makes: 2 to 3 servings

Prep Time: 15 minutes

Cook Time: 45 minutes to 1 hour

Ingredients

Pheasant

» 1 whole pheasant, cleaned
» 2 bacon strips

Red Currant Stuffing

» 1 apple
» ½ pound ground sausage
» 1 egg
» 1 teaspoon dried parsley flakes
» ½ teaspoons salt
» ½ teaspoons pepper
» 2 tablespoons red currant jelly

Wine Sauce

» ¼ cup butter
» ½ to 1 cup dry red wine
» 1 tablespoon red currant jelly
» Juice of ½ lemon

Preparation

1. Wipe the plucked and cleaned pheasant, inside and out, with a damp cloth. Preheat the oven to 350°F.

2. **Prepare the Red Currant Stuffing.** Core and chop the apple. In a medium bowl, combine the apple, sausage, egg, parsley flakes, salt, pepper, and 2 tablespoons of red currant jelly and mix well. Stuff the pheasant with the Red Currant Stuffing.

3. Place the stuffed pheasant, breast side up, on a rack in a roasting pan. Drape the strips of bacon over the pheasant breast. Roast the pheasant in the oven for 30 to 35 minutes.

4. **Prepare the Wine Sauce.** in a medium saucepan over low heat, combine the butter, wine, red currant jelly, and lemon juice. Heat, stirring often, until the sauce is melted and smooth.

Red currant jelly adds a unique and delicious flavor.

5. Remove the pheasant from the oven after the internal temperature at the thigh reaches 160°F; drain and discard the drippings from the pan. Pour the Wine Sauce over the pheasant. Return the pheasant to the oven for an additional 15 to 30 minutes, or until the pheasant is tender. Baste every 10 minutes with the sauce in the pan.

6. To serve, place the pheasant on a platter. Remove the stuffing from the pheasant and transfer it to a baking dish. If the stuffing registers below 165°F on a meat thermometer, return the dish to the oven until the temperature of the stuffing reaches at least 165°F. Carve the pheasant and serve with the stuffing on the side.

Easy Creamed Pheasant

After a little preparation time, pop this dish in the oven and check back in an hour or so and notice how the kitchen is filled with an enticing aroma. At 45 minutes or so, and with the simplest of ingredients, this preparation is one of the shortest and easiest routes from wild game harvest to delicious meal you can take.

Ingredients

» ½ cup flour
» 2 whole pheasant breasts, cut into ¼-inch pieces
» ½ cup butter
» ¼ cup chopped onion
» Salt and pepper, to taste
» 2 cups sour cream
» ¼ cup chopped fresh parsley
» Toast or biscuits, to serve

Makes: 4 servings
Prep Time: 10 minutes
Cook Time: 45 minutes

Preparation

1. Preheat the oven to 350°F. Place the flour in a large shallow dish and dredge the pheasant pieces in the flour.

2. In a large skillet over medium-high heat, melt the butter. Add the coated pheasant pieces and onion to the skillet and sauté until the onions are softened. Sprinkle with salt and pepper. Once the onions are tender and the pheasant pieces are browned, transfer the mixture to a 9-inch-square glass baking dish. Spread the sour cream over the pheasant and sprinkle with the chopped parsley. Cover the baking dish and bake for 45 minutes.

3. To serve, spoon the creamed pheasant mixture over toast or open-faced biscuits on each serving plate.

Hunting dogs will be happy with their pheasant catches.

Pheasant with Wild Rice

Some cooks stuff their pheasants with the mistaken notion that the stuffing will add flavor and moisture to the cooked bird. On the contrary, stuffing actually encourages overcooking and a dry pheasant. Cook the legs first, then the breasts. When done properly, the legs will pull off the bone easily and the breasts will be moist and tender.

Ingredients

- » 2 whole pheasants, cleaned
- » 1 cup wild rice
- » 1 teaspoon salt
- » ½ small onion
- » ½ green bell pepper
- » 1 stalk celery
- » One 4-ounce can chopped mushrooms
- » ¼ teaspoon pepper
- » 1 cup chicken broth
- » 4 bacon strips
- » ½ cup butter, melted

Makes: 4 to 6 servings

Prep Time: 20 minutes

Cook Time: 2 hours and 30 minutes

Preparation

1. Wipe the plucked and cleaned pheasants, inside and out, with a damp cloth. Starting at the breastbone, remove the breast fillets. Remove the legs at the body. Save the carcass for soup stock.

2. Bring 1 quart of water to a boil in a large saucepan over medium-high heat. Add the wild rice and salt. Reduce the heat to low, cover the saucepan, and let the rice simmer for 40 minutes.

3. Meanwhile, mince the onion, bell pepper, and celery. Drain the chopped mushrooms. Preheat the oven to 325°F.

4. Drain any unabsorbed water from the rice and spread the rice onto paper towels to dry. Transfer the cooked, dried rice to a medium lightly greased baking dish and add the onion, green bell pepper, and celery. Add the mushrooms and season with the pepper; mix well. Place the baking dish in the oven and bake for 20 minutes, then set aside for serving.

5. Place the legs in a roasting pan and add the chicken broth. Place the pan in the oven and bake for 2 hours, turning the legs once to brown both sides evenly. Place the breasts in the roasting pan and drape 2 strips of bacon over each pheasant breast. Roast the breasts in the oven for about 2½ hours or until the pheasant is tender. Baste the pheasants every 30 minutes with the melted butter and pan drippings.

6. To serve, slice the breasts into ½"-thick slices and garnish with the cooked legs. Serve with the wild rice stuffing on the side.

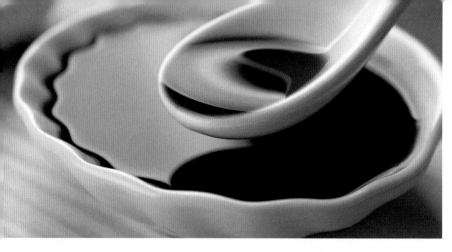

Homemade teriyaki sauce is always better than store-bought.

Teriyaki Pheasant

Making teriyaki sauce from scratch is better than anything you can get from something in a bottle at the store. Prepared teriyaki sauce from the market is often sweetened with corn syrup and tends to burn easily, causing a bitter taste; this recipe, on the other hand, has whole, fresh ingredients that result in a sauce that brings out the best from the pheasant.

Ingredients

Pheasants

» 2 pheasants, cut into serving pieces
» ¼ cup salt

Teriyaki Sauce

» 3 garlic cloves
» ¼ cups vegetable oil
» ½ cup sugar
» 2 tablespoons peeled and minced fresh ginger
» 1 cup dry white wine
» 1 cup soy sauce, plus more as needed
» 1 teaspoon mustard powder

Makes: 4 servings

Prep Time: 15 minutes, plus 4 hours and 30 minutes marinating

Cook Time: 1 hour and 30 minutes

Preparation

1. Place the pheasant pieces in a large bowl. Sprinkle salt over the pheasant pieces and add enough water to cover the pheasant. Cover the bowl and place it in the refrigerator for at least 4 hours.

2. **Prepare the Teriyaki Sauce.** Mince the garlic. In a small bowl, combine the garlic, vegetable oil, sugar, ginger, white wine, soy sauce, and mustard powder and mix well.

3. Rinse the pheasant pieces under cool running water and place them in a clean bowl. Pour the Teriyaki Sauce over the pheasant and return the pheasant to the refrigerator for 30 minutes to marinate.

4. Preheat the oven to 300°F. Remove the bowl from the refrigerator and transfer the pheasant pieces to a baking dish. Discard the marinade. Roast the pheasant uncovered for 1½ to 2 hours or until the meat is fork-tender. Baste every 30 minutes with additional soy sauce.

Savory Roasted Pheasant

Pheasant breasts cook much faster than the sinewy legs and thighs so it's a good idea to give the legs and thighs a one-hour head start before adding the breasts. With a harvested pheasant roasting in the oven with savory spices, the whole house will have an incredible aroma that will be impossible not to love.

Ingredients

- » 2 pheasants, cut into serving pieces
- » ¼ cup flour
- » 2 teaspoons salt, divided
- » 1 teaspoon pepper, plus 1 pinch
- » Pinch paprika
- » 2 tablespoons butter
- » 2 medium onions
- » ½ cup sweet vermouth
- » 1 teaspoon tomato paste
- » ⅛ teaspoon ground cinnamon
- » Butter, as needed
- » Toast, buttered and cut into triangles, to serve (optional)
- » Sprigs of fresh parsley, to serve (optional)

Makes: 4 to 6 servings

Prep Time: 10 to 15 minutes

Cook Time: 1 hour and 10 minutes

Preparation

1. Place the pheasant pieces in a large bowl. In a small bowl, combine the flour, 1 teaspoon of salt, 1 teaspoon of pepper, and paprika and mix well. Pour the flour mixture over the pheasant pieces in the bowl and turn until all the pieces are evenly dusted.

2. Preheat the oven to 350°F. In a large skillet over medium-high heat, melt the butter. Cook the pheasant pieces in the butter until they are evenly browned on all sides. Transfer the pheasant pieces to a roasting pan.

3. Dice the onions and add them to the skillet over medium heat. Stir in the sweet vermouth, tomato paste, cinnamon, the remaining 1 teaspoon of salt, and a pinch of pepper. Sauté for about 2 minutes or until the onions are translucent and tender. Pour the sautéed onion mixture around the pheasant pieces in the roasting pan.

4. Dot pieces of butter over the pheasant and place the roasting pan in the oven. Roast for 1 hour or until the pheasant meat is tender.

5. To serve, arrange the roasted pheasant pieces in a serving dish. Spoon some of the sauce from the pan over the pheasant. If desired, arrange buttered toast triangles in the dish and garnish with sprigs of fresh parsley.

It's helpful to know which pieces of the bird cook the fastest.

Quail & Goat Cheese–Stuffed Poblano Chiles

Not just good for quail, try this recipe with any upland game bird or even rabbits. Preparing the poblanos takes a bit of time up front, but the results are worth it. What better way is there to serve game bird than with goat cheese and tequila?

Ingredients

- » 8 large poblano chiles
- » 4 green onions
- » 2 garlic cloves
- » 2 tablespoons olive oil
- » 8 whole quail breasts, cut into ¼-inch pieces
- » 1 tablespoon tequila
- » ⅛ to ¼ teaspoon dried cilantro
- » 1 pound goat cheese
- » Salsa, to serve
- » Fresh cilantro, to serve
- » 1 lime, cut into 8 wedges, to garnish

Makes: 8 servings

Prep Time: 20 minute

Cook Time: 25 minutes

Preparation

1. Start by roasting the chiles. Using long tongs, hold each pepper over a gas flame and turn until the skin of the pepper is evenly charred. Or, place the peppers on a baking sheet and roast under the broiler, turning to darken all sides but being careful not to burn. Transfer the peppers to a sealable plastic bag. Seal the bag and let the peppers steam, allowing them to cool. Wear rubber gloves to carefully peel the skin from the cooled chiles. Make an incision down the side of each of the chiles and remove all the seeds.

2. Preheat the oven to 350°F. Chop the white and green part of the green onions and mince the garlic. Heat the olive oil in a large skillet over medium-high heat. Sauté the green onions, garlic, and quail until the onions are tender and the quail is browned.

3. Remove the pan from heat and keep it a safe distance from any open flame. Deglaze the skillet by stirring in the tequila. Once the ingredients have cooled to room temperature, stir in the cilantro and goat cheese and mix until evenly combined.

4. Carefully stuff the quail-and–goat cheese mixture into the roasted poblanos. If desired, the peppers can be sewn closed using strips of blanched leeks and a needle. Place the peppers, stuffed side up, on a baking sheet and cover with aluminum foil. Bake in the oven for 20 minutes. Uncover and carefully turn the peppers so any liquids leak out. Return the peppers to the oven and roast uncovered for 5 additional minutes.

5. To serve, place a small pool of salsa on each serving plate and sprinkle with cilantro leaves. Place one stuffed pepper over the salsa on each plate. Garnish with a lime wedge on the side.

Roasting the poblano carefully over the fire directly will get the best smoky flavor.

Game Bird Pot Pie

This dish can be made with a combination of upland game breasts or one species only. Many a hunting lodge pantry is stocked with an assortment of salty canned soup concentrates. But when you make the pot pie filling yourself, it is so much better. For the chopped game bird meat, 1-inch pieces are best. For best results, you want your pastry dough to be golden brown at the top.

You want your pastry dough to be golden brown at the top.

Makes: 4 servings
Prep Time: 10 to 15 minutes
Cook Time: 35 to 40 minutes

Ingredients

» 2 tablespoons olive oil
» 2½ cups chopped game bird breast meat
» Salt and pepper, to taste
» 3 tablespoons butter
» ¼ cup diced carrot
» ¼ cup diced celery
» ¼ cup diced onion
» 2 tablespoons all-purpose flour
» 1 cup half-and-half
» ¼ cup dry white wine
» 14 ounces basic pastry dough, divided in half and rolled into two 12-inch circles
» 6 strips bacon, cooked and crumbled
» 1½ cups quartered artichoke hearts
» ½ teaspoon kosher salt
» ¼ teaspoon cracked peppercorns
» 8 ounces shredded jack cheese
» 1 egg, beaten with ½ teaspoon cold water

Preparation

1. Heat the olive oil in a large skillet over medium-high heat. Season the meat with salt and pepper and lightly brown in the skillet.

2. Add the butter, carrot, celery, and onion to the skillet and sauté for 3 to 4 minutes. Sprinkle the flour over the vegetables and meat and cook for 2 to 3 minutes while stirring. Stir in a few tablespoons of half-and-half and continue adding and stirring until all of the half-and-half is incorporated and the mixture is smooth. Stir in the wine. Remove the pan from heat and allow the mixture to cool.

3. Preheat the oven to 400°F. Place one of the pastry circles in the bottom of a lightly greased pie pan. Combine the bacon, artichoke hearts, salt, and pepper in a bowl and arrange the mixture on the pastry. Sprinkle the cheese over top. Pour the cooled game bird meat sauce over top and top with the remaining pastry circle. Crimp the top edges together then trim and discard any excess pastry. Brush the top with the egg mixture.

4. Bake in the oven for 35 to 40 minutes or until the top is golden brown and the sauce is bubbly. Allow the pot pie to cool for 3 to 4 minutes before serving.

Roasted Wild Turkey

A whole roasted wild turkey looks great in a photo, but cooking the whole bird doesn't make much culinary sense. The legs require at least 2 hours more cooking time than the breasts. If you cook the breasts until the thighs are done, they will be dry and less flavorful, so roast the legs separately. When stuffing, pack loosely so that the breasts cook from both inside and outside.

Preparation

1. **Prepare the Stuffing.** In a large skillet over medium-high heat, fry the bacon strips until they are crisp. Remove the bacon and set them aside on paper towels to drain, reserving the bacon drippings in the skillet. Chop the onion and celery stalks and add them to the skillet. Sauté until the onion begins to soften.

2. Stir the red wine and chicken broth into the skillet with the onion and celery. Place the stuffing mix in a medium bowl. Pour the sautéed onion mixture and liquid from the skillet into the bowl and mix well. If the stuffing is too dry, add a little hot water and fluff with a fork. Crumble the cooked bacon and stir it into the stuffing mix.

3. Preheat the oven to 300°F. Rinse the turkey in cold water. Remove the legs at the body. Using paper towels, thoroughly pat dry both the outside and inside cavity of the turkey. Season all parts liberally with salt and pepper. Stuff the breast cavity with the Stuffing and stitch the turkey closed with kitchen twine or poultry pins.

4. Place the legs in the roasting pan, add chicken broth until it reaches about ½ inch up the sides of the pan, and cover with a lid or foil. Roast for 2 hours, making sure that there is always about ½ inch of broth in the pan.

5. Remove the roasting pan from the oven and remove the turkey legs from the pan. Add the stuffed turkey breast to the same roasting pan and drape the bacon strips over the turkey breast. Cover the roasting pan with a double layer of aluminum foil. Place the pan in the oven and roast for 2½ hours.

6. Remove the foil and pour the wine over the turkey breast. Return the pan to the oven and cook uncovered for an additional 45 minutes, basting every 15 minutes with the pan drippings. Remove the stuffing from the bird and place it in a baking dish. Continue to cook the stuffing in the oven until it reaches a temperature of at least 165°F.

7. To serve, carve the breast fillets into slices and place on a platter with the legs. Serve the stuffing on the side.

Makes: 8 to 10 servings

Prep Time: 20 minutes

Cook Time: 3 hours and 30 minutes to 4 hours

Ingredients

Stuffing
» ½ pound bacon strips
» 1 medium onion
» 2 celery stalks
» ½ cup dry red wine
» ¾ cup chicken broth
» One 6-ounce package of turkey stuffing mix

Turkey
» One 10- to 15-pound wild turkey
» Salt and pepper, to taste
» Chicken broth, as needed
» ½ pound bacon strips
» ½ cup dry white wine

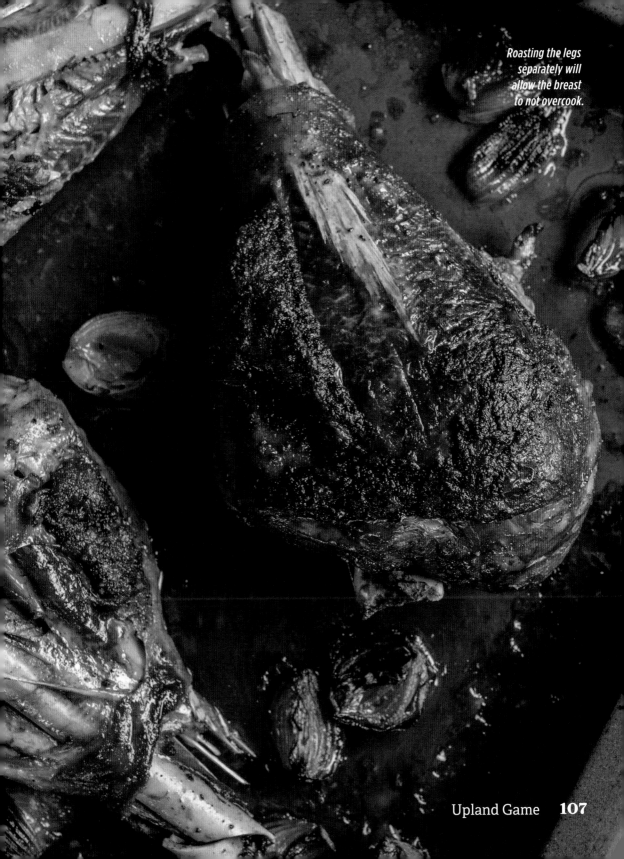

Roasting the legs separately will allow the breast to not overcook.

Stuffed Wild Turkey Breast

One of the ways to discourage your wild turkey breast from being dry and overcooked is to stuff it with vegetables and cheese, and it's the cheese added to the stuffing that makes this an instant comfort meal. Whenever you stuff cheese into a piece of meat, add some breadcrumbs to keep the cheese from running out when it heats up.

Makes: 4 servings

Prep Time:
10 to 15 minutes

Cook Time:
12 to 15 minutes

Ingredients

Sausage Stuffing

» 1 cup ground wild boar sausage
» ⅓ cup diced onion
» 1½ cups mushrooms, quartered

Turkey Breast

» 1 wild turkey breast
» Salt and pepper, to taste
» ¼ cup fresh basil leaves
» ⅓ cup shredded jack cheese
» 2 tablespoons breadcrumbs
» Olive oil, as needed
» 2 cups cherry tomatoes, halved, to serve
» 2 avocados, peeled, seeded, and diced, to serve

Preparation

1. Cut a pocket into the turkey breast. Season the turkey liberally inside and out with salt and pepper.

2. **Prepare the Sausage Stuffing.** In a large skillet over medium heat, cook the sausage for 2 to 3 minutes. Add the onion and mushrooms and cook until the sausage is just cooked and the onions are translucent. Allow the mixture to cool completely.

3. Stuff the Sausage Stuffing mixture into the pocket in the turkey breast. Add the basil. Combine the cheese with the breadcrumbs and stuff it into the pocket. Roll the turkey breast up while tucking in the ends, much like rolling a burrito. Place the turkey seam side down (where the edges meet) in a lightly oiled baking dish or Dutch oven. (Placing with the edge down will allow the turkey breast to seal when cooking.) If desired, secure the edges with butcher string or wooden skewers. Preheat the oven to 350°F.

4. Roast the turkey in the oven (or on a stovetop over medium-low heat) until the turkey breast is lightly browned on the bottom. Carefully flip it over and brown on the other side. The internal temperature should be 145°F when done. Remove the turkey from the dish or Dutch oven and allow it to rest for 5 for 7 minutes. Slice it into 1-to-2-inch medallions, arrange them on a platter, and top with tomato and avocado.

The cheese added to the stuffing makes this an instant comfort meal.

Chicken-Fried Wild Turkey Breast

This is a great snack for ballgames, picnics, or after school for the kids. If your turkey is an old Tom, you might want to tenderize the strips of meat by pounding them with a mallet or heavy skillet. Italian dressing has been used as a game marinade for decades. If you want to make this extra special, use the Italian marinade recipe in the last chapter of this book.

Ingredients

- » 1 whole wild turkey breast
- » One 16-ounce bottle Italian dressing
- » ½ teaspoon salt, plus ¼ teaspoon, and more to taste
- » ½ teaspoon pepper, plus ¼ teaspoon, and more to taste
- » 2 eggs
- » 3 cups milk, divided
- » 2 cups flour, plus 2 tablespoons
- » ¼ teaspoon salt
- » ¼ teaspoon pepper
- » Peanut or vegetable oil, for frying
- » 2 tablespoons butter, melted

Makes: 4 serving

Prep Time:
15 minutes, plus
8 hours marinating

Cook Time:
10 to 15 minutes

Preparation

1. Debone the turkey breast and cut the meat into strips across the grain. In a medium bowl, combine the Italian dressing, ½ teaspoon of salt, and ½ teaspoon of pepper and mix well. Add the turkey strips to the bowl, turning until evenly coated. Place the bowl in the refrigerator for 8 hours or overnight to marinate.

2. Beat the eggs in a small bowl. Add 2 cups of milk and whisk the eggs and milk together. In a separate bowl, combine 2 cups of flour, ¼ teaspoon of salt, and ¼ teaspoon of pepper and mix well. Remove the turkey strips from the refrigerator and discard the marinade. Dip the marinated turkey strips first into the egg mixture and then into the flour mixture.

3. Heat ¼ to ½ inch of oil in a large skillet over medium-high heat. Once the oil is hot, carefully place the coated turkey strips in the skillet and fry until golden brown, turning once. Remove the turkey strips and set them aside on paper towels to drain, reserving the oil in the skillet for the gravy.

4. To prepare the gravy, add 2 tablespoons of flour to the remaining oil and drippings in the skillet. Whisk in the melted butter and season with a pinch of salt and a pinch of pepper. Slowly whisk in 1 cup of milk, stirring constantly until the gravy is thick.

5. To serve, place the fried turkey strips on serving plates. Drizzle the gravy over the turkey or serve the gravy on the side.

This dish makes for a great snack or light meal.

Southwestern Rabbit

Younger rabbits are better table fare than the older ones. Mature, sinewy bunnies are best cooked low and slow, with moist heat. Either way, when the meat is done, it should just about fall off the bone.

Makes: 4 servings

Prep Time: 15 to 20 minutes

Cook Time: 1 hour and 15 minutes

Ingredients

- » ½ cup vegetable oil, plus 2 tablespoons
- » 2 rabbits, cut into serving pieces
- » 1 medium onion
- » 3 celery stalks
- » 1 green bell pepper
- » 1 tablespoon chili powder
- » 1 cup ketchup
- » 2 tablespoons brown sugar
- » ½ tablespoon ground cumin
- » 2 tablespoons Worcestershire sauce
- » 1 teaspoon salt

Preparation

1. Place ½ cup of vegetable oil in a large skillet over medium-high heat. Once the oil is hot, brown the rabbit pieces on all sides. Transfer the browned rabbit pieces to a 9 x 13–inch glass baking dish.

2. Preheat the oven to 350°F. Chop the onion, celery, and green bell pepper. In the same skillet, add another 2 tablespoons of vegetable oil. Stir in the onion, celery, and green bell pepper. Add the chili powder, ketchup, brown sugar, cumin, Worcestershire sauce, salt, and 1 cup of water. Mix well and bring the mixture to a boil. Pour the sauce over the rabbit pieces in the baking dish.

3. Place the baking dish in the oven. Bake covered for 30 minutes. Turn the rabbit pieces over, remove the cover, and bake for an additional 30 minutes or until the rabbit is tender. Make sure that there is always about ½ inch of liquid in the baking dish, adding additional water as needed.

Rabbits at different ages will need to be cooked differently.

Fajita tortillas are smaller than those used for other dishes.

Rabbit Fajitas

A word of caution when handling and cooking wild rabbits: Tularemia or "rabbit fever" is most common during warm weather months; it's important to always cook rabbit meat to an internal temperature of 165°F. Wear rubber gloves when processing the animals and make sure to thoroughly sanitize all knives and cutting surfaces. Look at the last chapter of the book for a world of ideas for great salsas to pair with the fajitas.

Makes: 2 to 4 servings
Prep Time: 15 minutes
Cook Time: 30 minutes

Ingredients

» 1 rabbit, cut into serving pieces
» 1 teaspoon salt, plus more to taste
» 4 tablespoons olive oil, divided
» 2 red bell peppers
» 1 large onion
» 2 garlic cloves
» Fajita-size tortillas, to serve
» Sour cream, to serve
» Salsa, to serve

Preparation

1. Season the rabbit pieces with salt to taste. Place 2 tablespoons of olive oil in a large skillet over medium-high heat. Once the oil is hot, add the rabbit pieces and brown them on all sides. Continue to cook until the rabbit meat is cooked through. Remove the cooked rabbit pieces and set them aside on a plate to cool.

2. Cut the red bell peppers into thin slices, chop the onion, and mince the garlic. Once the rabbit meat has cooled slightly, pull the meat from the bone and shred. Place the remaining 2 tablespoons of olive oil in the skillet. Place the rabbit meat, pepper slices, onion, and garlic in the skillet. Sprinkle the salt over top and sauté until the vegetables are tender.

3. To serve, spoon the desired amount of rabbit meat and vegetables onto each fajita tortilla. Top each with a dollop of sour cream and salsa. Roll up the fajitas and serve.

Rabbit in Cream Sauce

Rabbit meat is similar to chicken but much leaner, which makes the heavy cream sauce of this preparation the perfect complement to the meat.

Ingredients

- » 1 rabbit, cut into serving pieces
- » Salt, to taste
- » ½ cup flour, plus 1 ½ tablespoons
- » 2 tablespoons vegetable oil
- » 2 medium onions
- » 2 slices lemon
- » ½ teaspoon dried oregano
- » 1 bay leaf
- » ¼ teaspoon pepper
- » 3 tablespoons red wine vinegar
- » 1 tablespoon butter
- » 2 cups sour cream
- » ½ teaspoon sugar
- » Potatoes, boiled, to serve (optional)

Makes: 4 servings

Prep Time: 15 minutes

Cook Time:
1 hour and 15 minutes

Preparation

1. Season the rabbit pieces with salt and dredge them in ½ cup of flour. Place the vegetable oil in a large skillet over medium-high heat. Once the oil is hot, add the rabbit pieces and brown them on all sides.

2. Chop the onions. Add the onions, lemon slices, oregano, bay leaf, and pepper to the skillet. Add the red wine vinegar and simmer, stirring often, until the rabbit is tender, about 50 to 60 minutes.

3. Remove the rabbit pieces and set them aside, keeping them warm in the oven. Add the butter and 1½ tablespoons of flour to the skillet. Stir the mixture into a roux, then stir in the sour cream and sugar. Bring the roux to a light simmer and remove the bay leaf. If the sauce is too thick, add a little water.

4. To serve, place the rabbit pieces on serving plates and drizzle with the cream sauce or serve with boiled potatoes and the sauce on the side.

A warm slice of crusty bread to mop up the remaining cream is the best side for this dish.

Couscous is one of many great side options for this wholesome dish.

Sautéed Quail with Mushrooms

Quail recipes often instruct cooks to cook the quail until the juices run clear, but if you wait for the juices to run clear, there won't be any juices. When properly cooked, quail should still be just a little pink at the thigh joint. Once removed from the heat source, quail will continue to cook. Couscous is one of many great side options for this wholesome dish but you can also use noodles or rice or experiment with side dishes of your choice.

Makes: 2 to 4 servings

Prep Time: 15 minutes

Cook Time:
   35 to 40 minutes

Ingredients

» 4 whole quail, plucked and cleaned
» 2 lemons
» Salt and pepper, to taste
» ¼ cup butter
» One 16-ounce package whole fresh mushrooms
» ½ cup white wine
» Fresh parsley sprigs, as needed
» Couscous, to serve (optional)

Preparation

1. Wipe the plucked and cleaned quail, inside and out, with a damp cloth.

2. Cut each lemon in half. Rub the cut side of one lemon half over each quail. Season the inside and outside of each quail with salt and pepper.

3. In a large skillet over medium-high heat, melt the butter. Add the quail and mushrooms to the skillet. Brown the quail on all sides while sautéing the mushrooms.

4. Once the quail are nicely browned, add the white wine and several fresh parsley sprigs. Cover the skillet and simmer for 5 to 10 minutes or until the quail are just cooked.

5. To serve, place each quail on a serving plate. Discard any wilted parsley sprigs. Spoon the mushrooms and sauce from the skillet over each quail. Garnish with fresh parsley sprigs and serve with couscous, if using.

Skillet Pheasant Breasts

Compared to chicken, pheasants are much leaner and cook much quicker. In fact, pheasants cook quite quickly, so it's essential to keep an eye on your skillet and make sure to use the right amount of cooking oil, because it only takes a couple of minutes extra to overcook pheasant breasts. You can prepare the pheasant with the skin on or off, to your preference.

Makes: 4 servings

Prep Time:
   10 to 15 minutes

Cook Time:
   12 to 15 minutes

Pheasants cook quickly, so keep an eye on your skillet and make sure to use the right amount of cooking oil.

Ingredients

- » 4 to 6 boneless pheasant breast halves
- » ¼ cup olive oil, divided
- » Salt and pepper, to taste
- » 2 garlic cloves, minced
- » 3 finely diced tablespoons onion
- » 2 tablespoons capers
- » 1 teaspoon Dijon mustard
- » ¼ cup white wine vinegar
- » Pinch sugar
- » ¼ cup chopped black olives
- » 1 cup quartered small tomatoes
- » ¼ cup chopped fresh basil or parsley leaves
- » ⅓ cup shredded Parmesan cheese, to top

Preparation

1. Rub the pheasant meat with 2 tablespoons olive oil and season with salt and pepper. Heat 1 tablespoon oil in a large skillet over medium-high heat. Add the meat and lightly brown it on both sides. Add garlic, onion, capers, mustard, white wine vinegar, and sugar. Cook for 2 to 3 minutes. Remove the pheasant when it is just cooked and set it aside, keeping it warm in the oven.

2. Whisk in the remaining olive oil. Add the olives, tomatoes, and basil and season with salt and pepper to taste.

3. Spoon the tomato mixture over the cooked pheasant breasts and top with the Parmesan cheese.

Waterfowl

Duck is a classic waterfowl, and for good reason, since it's so versatile.

Too many duck hunters are passionate about the hunt, but not so enthusiastic about cooking and eating their catch. How we prepare ducks and geese has changed dramatically over the past few decades. It used to be standard practice to stuff ducks and geese with wild rice, fruits, and vegetables, with the delusional belief that the stuffing would remove some of the gamey flavors. It does not.

Ducks and geese are best cooked in parts unless the goal is to cook it until it falls off the bone. Prepared duck and goose meat can be used in soups, stews, tacos, and barbecue. It makes for wonderful sandwiches as well as entrée dishes that wow dinner guests. If you prefer meat that is cooked all the way through, duck and goose are good options. If you prefer a juicy, medium-rare duck, first remove the breast fillets and cook the legs longer, as the legs are not edible at medium-rare.

Pre-brine Your Duck or Goose for Best Results

Prior to preparing a duck or goose dinner, it is best to brine them in a mild saltwater solution called a brine. A basic brine is 2 quarts water mixed with ½ cup of coarse salt like kosher salt or sea salt. Brining removes any excess liquids and replaces them with the brine. Start with the water and salt in a saucepan over low heat and stir until the salt is dissolved. If you want to add additional flavors like garlic, onion, or herbs that will enhance the flavor of the cooked birds, feel free to do so, but do not add additional liquids—the salt-to-water ratio needs to be correct or the brine will not pass through the meat. For those who do not like "bloody" meat, note that the bloody-looking liquid in duck or goose is not blood. It is myoglobin, an oxygen-binding protein found mostly in the muscles of animals.

On Puddlers vs. Divers

Puddlers like mallards, pintail, and wigeon are known for being milder in flavor than darker-fleshed divers and sea ducks. Depending on the time of year and location, puddle ducks can have a nice layer of fat which will enhance the flavor of the meat. When cooking a mallard breast with the skin intact, start by placing the breast skin side down in a medium skillet. The plan is to render down the fat under the skin and then finish the breast in its own liquified fat.

Once browned on the skin side, flip it over, crank up the heat, and continue cooking to the desired internal temperature. Just before serving, return the skin side to the skillet to crisp it up before serving. Top with a drizzle of your favorite sauce or a tablespoon of butter.

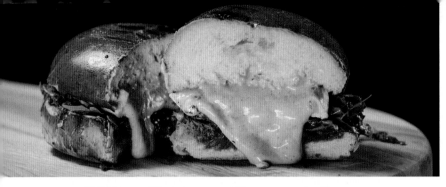

A classic burger includes lettuce, tomato, and cheese. If you're not a fan of blue cheese, try using your favorite type instead.

Grilled Duck & Blue Cheese Sandwich

This classic duck burger sandwich proves that duck isn't just for dinner. When cooked properly, the meat can be used for just about any recipe that calls for beef. If you are preparing a smaller duck species that you have harvested, simply prepare more ducks. The blue cheese sauce elevates this sandwich to decadent, delicious heights.

Makes: 2 to 4 servings

Prep Time: 1 5 minutes, plus 8 hours marinating

Cook Time: 20 to 25 minutes

Ingredients

Duck Seasoning
» 1 tablespoon kosher salt
» 1 teaspoon coarsely ground black pepper
» 1 teaspoon Italian seasoning
» 1 teaspoon onion powder

Blue Cheese Sauce
» 8 ounces crumbled blue cheese
» 2 tablespoons butter
» ¼ cup beer
» Dash Tabasco sauce

Sandwiches
» 6 skinless duck breast fillets
» 1 large onion, cut into thick rings
» 2 tablespoons olive oil
» Salt and pepper, to taste
» 1 large tomato, cut into 4 slices
» 4 sturdy burger buns
» 4 lettuce leaves

Preparation

1. Place the duck breasts on a firm surface and, while pressing down gently on the top of each breast, slice each in half widthwise between your hand and the surface. Keep your fingertips up and away from the knife blade! You'll have 12 slices.

2. **Prepare the Duck Seasoning.** Combine the kosher salt, pepper, Italian seasoning, and onion powder and rub the mixture onto the sliced ducks, on both sides. Stack the seasoned meat together, wrap it all snugly with plastic wrap, and refrigerate it for 1 to 4 hours.

3. **Prepare the Blue Cheese Sauce.** In a small saucepan over low heat, combine the blue cheese, butter, beer, and Tabasco, stirring constantly until the mixture is smooth. Set aside and keep the sauce warm in the oven.

4. Coat the onion slices with olive oil, salt, and pepper. Place the onions on a medium-hot, well-lubricated grill and cook for 5 minutes. Place the seasoned duck slices on the grill and cook for 2 to 3 minutes per side for medium-rare.

5. To assemble the sandwiches, arrange lettuce and tomato on the bottom of each bun. Top with 3 slices of duck breast and some of the grilled onions. Top with warm blue cheese sauce and the other half of the bun and serve.

Sweet Jalapeño Grilled Duck

This recipe has just enough heat to get your attention, but not enough to hurt you. The marinade and glaze are mildly hot, a little sweet, and bring just enough sour to achieve balance. To get the tenderest duck legs, get the legs baking for two to three hours before you grill the breasts. See the last chapter of the book for plenty of ideas for salsas to serve this recipe with.

Makes: 4 to 6 servings

Prep Time: 10 minutes, plus 6 to 12 hours marinating

Cook Time: 10 to 12 minutes

Adding jalapeño slices to the grill will boost your duck's flavor.

Ingredients

Sweet Jalapeño Marinade
» 2 cups water
» 2 cups orange juice concentrate
» ½ cup apple cider vinegar
» ½ cup vegetable oil
» 6 jalapeños, thinly sliced widthwise
» 6 garlic cloves, minced
» ¼ cup freshly squeezed lime juice
» ¼ cup sugar
» 2 tablespoons kosher salt
» 1 teaspoon ground cumin

Duck
» 4 whole ducks
» Flour or corn tortillas, warmed, to serve
» Mild tomato salsa, to serve

Preparation

1. Place the ducks breast side up on a firm surface. With a sharp, thin-bladed knife, slice along each side of the breastbone to remove the breasts from the carcass. Work the knife toward the back of each side and remove the legs at the joint where the thighs connect to the body.

2. **Prepare the Sweet Jalapeño Marinade**. Combine all of the ingredients in a large bowl (plastic, ceramic, or glass) and mix well. Reserve 1 cup of the marinade to use as a baste while grilling. Place the ducks in the remaining marinade and refrigerate for 6 to 12 hours, turning occasionally.

3. Remove the ducks from the marinade and lace the breasts skin side down (if the skin is intact) on a medium-hot grill for approximately 4 to 5 minutes per side for medium-rare. If the legs were oven-baked in advance, grill them with the breasts until browned. While grilling, baste the meat occasionally with the reserved marinade.

4. Remove the ducks from the grill and let them rest for 5 minutes before serving. Serve with warm flour or corn tortillas and mild tomato salsa.

Duck Schnitzel with Mushroom Sauce

Everyone knows about veal or pork schnitzel but take your wild game cooking to the next level with duck (or even goose). Although the recipe doesn't call for it, try first brining the meat overnight in a brine of ½ gallon of cold water mixed with ½ cup kosher salt. The brining process eliminates any trace of bloody liquids once the meat is cooked. Once brined, rinse the meat, pat it dry, and then proceed with the recipe.

Ingredients

Mushroom Sauce

» 3 tablespoons butter
» 2 garlic cloves, minced
» ¼ cup minced onion
» 3 cups sliced mushrooms
» ¼ cup diced red bell pepper
» 1 teaspoon minced fresh rosemary
» 2 tablespoons flour
» 1 ½ cups chicken broth
» ½ teaspoon Dijon mustard

Duck Schnitzel

» 4 to 8 duck breast fillets, skin removed
» kosher salt, to taste
» Freshly ground black pepper, to taste
» 2 cups flour, seasoned with 1 teaspoon salt and 1 teaspoon pepper
» 6 eggs, whisked with ¼ cup buttermilk
» 2 cups seasoned breadcrumbs
» 3 tablespoons olive oil
» 2 tablespoons butter

Makes: 6 to 8 servings

Prep Time: 15 minutes

Cook Time: 12 to 15 minutes

Preparation

1. **Prepare the Mushroom Sauce.** Heat the butter in a medium saucepan over medium heat. Add the garlic and onion and sauté for 3 minutes. Add the mushrooms, bell pepper, and rosemary and sauté for 3 to 4 minutes. Sprinkle the flour over the mixture and stir to distribute evenly. Cook for 3 to 4 minutes, stirring often. Stir in the chicken broth and Dijon mustard. Then simmer, uncovered, until the sauce thickens. Remove the Mushroom Sauce from heat and keep it warm in the oven.

2. **Prepare the Duck Schnitzel.** Place the breast fillets inside a freezer bag or between sheets of plastic wrap and lightly pound the fillets with a mallet or heavy skillet until they are ¼ to ⅛ inch thick. Season with kosher salt and freshly ground pepper.

3. Place three shallow bowls on a work surface. Put the seasoned flour in the first bowl, the egg mixture in the second, and the breadcrumbs in the third. Heat the olive oil and butter in a large skillet over medium-high heat.

4. Dredge each duck breast fillet in the flour mixture first. Shake off any excess. Then dip the fillet in the egg mixture, coating the fillet evenly on all sides. Then press the fillet into the breadcrumbs, coating evenly. Shake off any excess. Then place the coated fillets, 1 or 2 at a time, into the skillet and brown them evenly on both sides. Remove the schnitzels and set them on paper towels to drain; keep them warm in the oven.

5. To serve, arrange the schnitzel on plates and spoon the Mushroom Sauce over.

This recipe works with
the breast meat of any
wild duck or goose you
may harvest.

Duck & Shrimp Gumbo

The way to achieving an amazing gumbo begins with preparing a great roux—a rich mixture of liquified fat and flour that thickens your gumbo, and which should be somewhere between blond-colored or peanut butter–colored to brown, mahogany-colored. In this recipe, the fat is vegetable oil. And be aware: if your gumbo has tomatoes, it's not gumbo. Ask anyone from Louisiana.

Makes: 6 to 8 servings

Prep Time: 20 minutes

Cook Time: 1 hour and 30 minutes to 2 hours

Ingredients

» 2 ducks, skin on, cut into serving pieces
» 1 tablespoon vegetable oil
» ½ cup flour
» 2 medium onions
» 2 celery stalks
» 1 large red bell pepper
» 1 large green bell pepper
» 4 bay leaves
» 2 teaspoons salt
» 6 cups chicken broth
» 6 green onions
» 1 pound medium shrimp, peeled and deveined
» ¼ teaspoon cayenne pepper

Preparation

1. Clean the duck pieces and pat them dry with paper towels. Prick the skin of the duck all over with the tip of a sharp knife.

2. In a large heavy pot over medium-high heat, heat the vegetable oil. Add the duck pieces in batches and brown them on all sides. Transfer the browned duck pieces to a bowl and discard all but ¼ cup of the pan drippings. Return the pot to medium-low heat. Stir the flour into the drippings in the pan to make a roux. Heat for about 10 minutes, stirring often, until the roux is well-browned, like the color of peanut butter or, if you prefer a more intense flavor, cook until the roux is more of a mahogany color, but be careful: as the roux darkens, it can burn in minutes. If it does burn, it can't be saved and you must start over.

3. Meanwhile, chop the onions, celery, and peppers. Stir the onions, celery, peppers, bay leaves, and salt into the pot. Heat, stirring occasionally, until the vegetables are tender but still crisp. Stir in 4 cups of water, the chicken broth, and the browned duck pieces. Bring the soup to a boil, reduce the heat, and let it simmer until the duck is tender, about 2 to 2½ hours.

4. Remove the soup from heat. Transfer the duck pieces to a cutting board and shred the meat into large pieces, discarding any bones and skin. Skim any fat from the surface of the soup.

5. Return the duck meat to the gumbo and bring the soup to a boil. Meanwhile, chop the green onion stems. Reduce the soup to a simmer and stir in the green onions, shrimp, and cayenne pepper and cook for about 2 minutes. Remove and discard the bay leaves before serving.

A good roux is the start to an amazing gumbo.

Italian Duck Sandwich

Duck camp is no place for sliders or a teaspoon of meat on a cracker, especially after a long day in the marsh. The beauty of this dish is that the time-consuming cooking component is done well in advance. Whole ducks or breast fillets are seasoned, slow-cooked, cooled, and shredded. If you don't want to use whole ducks, you can substitute six to eight duck breast fillets.

Ingredients

- » 2 tablespoons kosher salt
- » 1 tablespoon pepper
- » 2 tablespoons garlic powder
- » 2 tablespoons paprika
- » 3 tablespoons vegetable oil
- » 3 to 4 whole ducks, split in half, with backbones removed
- » 1 medium onion, roughly chopped
- » 1 tablespoon Italian seasoning

- » 2 teaspoons crushed red pepper
- » 6 garlic cloves, minced
- » 1 cup dry red wine
- » ½ cup red wine vinegar
- » 2 cups beef stock or broth
- » 6 sturdy sourdough or French rolls, split
- » Pepperoncini, sliced, to serve
- » Pickled hot or sweet peppers, to serve

Makes: 6 to 8 servings

Prep Time: 20 minutes, plus 1 to 8 hours marinating

Cook Time: 1 hour and 30 minutes to 2 hours

Preparation

1. In a small bowl or bag, combine the kosher salt, pepper, garlic powder, and paprika. Liberally coat the duck with this mixture. Cover and refrigerate for at least 1 hour, but preferably for 6 or more hours.

2. Heat the oil in a Dutch oven over medium-high heat. Add the duck and brown it evenly on all sides. Add the onion and cook for 5 minutes. Mix in the Italian seasoning, crushed red pepper, and garlic and cook for 2 minutes. Add the wine and stir to deglaze the bits stuck to the bottom of the pot. Add the vinegar and beef stock and bring the mixture to a boil. Reduce the heat to low, cover, and simmer for several hours, until the meat pulls apart easily. Remove the pot from heat.

Meat piled high on French rolls makes the best sandwich for an evening or afternoon meal.

3. Remove the duck from the pot and let it cool completely. Pull the meat off the bones or shred the breasts into bite-size pieces. Strain the liquid from the pot and add it to the pulled meat.

4. To serve, reheat the meat and liquid in a skillet or Dutch oven. Add the pepperoncini and peppers and bring them to serving temperature. Spoon the mixture onto rolls.

Dutch Oven Duck

Cooking in the Dutch oven on simmer will let those flavors sit and marinate just right. Whether your heat source is a bed of white-hot coals or a rustic camp stove, a Dutch oven can cook your duck to fall-off-the-bone deliciousness. It's an old-school slow cooker for meat dishes that require low cooking temperatures and a little more time to make them tender. The duck breast fillets should be cut into 1-inch cubes, as should be the sweet potato and russet potato.

Makes: 4 to 6 servings

Prep Time: 20 minutes

Cook Time:
2 hours and 30 minutes

Ingredients

» 3 cups chopped duck breast fillets
» kosher salt, to taste
» Freshly ground black pepper, to taste
» Olive or vegetable oil, as needed
» 1 large red onion, roughly chopped
» 3 medium carrots, roughly chopped
» 3 celery stalks, roughly chopped
» 1 bell pepper, diced
» 3 to 5 garlic cloves, minced
» 1½ quarts beef or chicken broth
» 1½ cups peeled and chopped sweet potato
» 1½ cups peeled and chopped russet potato
» 3 cups sliced fresh mushrooms
» 2 sprigs fresh rosemary
» Salt and pepper, to taste
» Crusty bread, to serve

Preparation

1. Season the duck liberally with salt and pepper. Heat a thin layer of oil in a Dutch oven over medium-high heat. Add the duck and brown it evenly on all sides. Mix in the onion, carrots, celery, and bell pepper. Cook, stirring often, until the onions are translucent.

2. Add the garlic and broth. Cover and simmer for 2 hours or until the meat is tender. Add the sweet potato, russet potato, mushrooms, and rosemary. Simmer for 15 to 20 minutes or until the potatoes are just cooked. Season to taste with salt and pepper. Serve with crusty bread.

Simmering in the Dutch oven will let your flavors sit and marinate just right.

Goose Breast à l'Orange

While duck (pictured) is typically used for this famous French cuisine entrée, goose makes an excellent substitute and a fun dish to try, especially if that's what you've been hunting. Although this is a somewhat simplified version of the venerable dish, it's still a winner. Grilling the meat outdoors will give the duck the most delicious sear. If you don't have Grand Marnier on hand, you can use any orange liqueur.

Makes:
2 to 4 servings

Prep Time:
15 to 20 minutes

Cook Time:
20 to 30 minutes

Ingredients

À l'Orange Sauce

» ½ cup frozen orange juice concentrate
» 1 tablespoon minced fresh ginger
» 2 tablespoons Grand Marnier
» 1 tablespoon soy sauce
» ½ cup duck or chicken broth
» 2 tablespoons brown sugar
» 2 tablespoons currant jelly
» 2 tablespoons butter
» Pinch salt
» Pinch pepper
» 1 tablespoon cornstarch

Goose Breasts

» 2 whole wild goose breasts
» Salt and pepper, to taste

Preparation

1. **Prepare the à l'Orange Sauce.** In a medium saucepan over medium heat, combine the orange juice concentrate, ginger, liqueur, soy sauce, and broth. Cook, stirring occasionally, until the liquid is reduced and becomes slightly syrupy. Stir in the brown sugar and jelly. Turn off the heat and mix in the butter, a pinch of salt, and a pinch of pepper. In a small glass, combine the cornstarch with 2 tablespoons water and mix well. Stir the cornstarch mixture into the sauce. The sauce will thicken as it sits.

2. Preheat an outdoor grill to medium-high heat. Debone and clean the goose breasts, then pat them dry with paper towels. Generously season both sides of the breasts with salt and pepper. Pound the breasts slightly with a meat mallet for even thickness. Grill the breasts until the meat is seared on both sides and cooked through to medium-rare or medium.

3. To serve, place the breasts on a platter and let them rest a few minutes before slicing. Carve the meat across the grain into ½-inch thick slices. Place the slices on serving plates and spoon a generous amount of the warmed À l'Orange Sauce over each serving.

While duck is typically used for this meal, goose makes an excellent substitute—and a fun twist to try.

Spicy Duck or Goose Wrap

The amount of spicy heat in this preparation can easily be adjusted down or eliminated altogether by removing the ribs and seeds from the jalapeño and reducing the amount of sriracha sauce in the marinade. The Herb Mayonnaise makes this lunch-friendly duck dish truly mouthwatering, but you can simplify the recipe if you're in a hurry. For the herbs, use any combination of parsley, basil, chives, oregano, or other garden-fresh herbs of your choice.

Ingredients

Spicy Marinade

» ½ cup low-sodium soy sauce
» 2 tablespoons sriracha sauce
» 2 tablespoons brown sugar
» 1 tablespoon freshly squeezed lime juice
» 1 jalapeño, sliced into rings
» 1 teaspoon black pepper
» 2 garlic cloves, minced
» 2 green onions, roughly chopped
» ½ cup olive oil

Herb Mayonnaise

» 2 large egg yolks
» ¾ teaspoon Dijon mustard
» 1 tablespoon freshly squeezed lemon juice
» 1 garlic clove, minced
» 1 cup vegetable oil
» ¼ cup finely chopped fresh herbs
» Salt and pepper, to taste

Wraps

» 2 cups skinless duck or goose breast fillets, sliced across the grain
» Olive or vegetable oil, as needed
» 4 large flour tortillas, to serve
» Lettuce, to serve
» Tomatoes, sliced, to serve
» Jack cheese, grated, to serve

Makes: 4 servings

Prep Time: 10 to 15 minutes

Cook Time: 10 minutes

Preparation

1. **Prepare the Spicy Marinade.** In a medium bowl, whisk together all the ingredients, except the olive oil. Add the olive oil in a thin stream, whisking until emulsified.

2. Add the sliced duck or goose to the Spicy Marinade, toss to coat evenly, cover, and refrigerate for 6 to 12 hours, turning occasionally.

3. **Prepare the Herb Mayonnaise.** Place the egg yolks, Dijon mustard, lemon juice, and garlic in a blender or food processor. Pulse to blend. With the motor running on low speed, add the vegetable oil in a thin stream until the mayonnaise is creamy. Add the herbs and season the mayo to taste with salt and pepper. Store in the refrigerator for up to 2 weeks.

4. Lightly oil a skillet over medium-high heat. Remove the sliced breast fillets from the Spicy Marinade, discarding the marinade, and pat them dry. Cook them in the skillet for 2 to 3 minutes or until they reach your desired doneness.

5. To serve, spread a layer of Herb Mayonnaise over each flour tortilla. Add the cooked breast fillets, lettuce, tomato, and cheese. Fold over the bottom and roll tightly.

This is a healthy lunch dish that can be quick if you don't want to make your Herb Mayonnaise from scratch.

Have all the veggies ready to be tossed in!

Duck Stir-Fry

Time is critical when preparing a stir-fry so be sure you have all the ingredients ready for dump-and-go time, when vegetables, meats, oils, and sauces have to be added to the wok in quick succession. The cooked duck will be tender. As always, slice the fillets against the grain. For those who don't know, ponzu is a Japanese dipping sauce combining soy sauce, citrus, and other ingredients. Both ponzu and unagi sauce can be found in Asian markets or online or even at your grocery store.

Ingredients

» 2 cups thinly sliced skinless duck breast fillets
» 1 tablespoon cornstarch
» ¼ cup ponzu
» ½ teaspoon sesame oil
» 3 tablespoons vegetable or peanut oil
» 4 green onions, roughly chopped
» 2 cups halved baby bok choy or shredded cabbage
» 1 cup thinly sliced celery
» ¼ cup unagi sauce
» 2 tablespoons minced pickled ginger
» 1 teaspoon sriracha sauce

Makes: 6 to 8 servings
Prep Time: 15 minutes
Cook Time: 10 minutes

Preparation

1. In a bowl, combine the sliced duck breast with cornstarch, ponzu, and sesame oil and toss to coat evenly, smoothing out any lumps from the cornstarch.

2. Heat the vegetable or peanut oil in a medium-hot skillet or wok. Add the duck and its soaking liquid and quickly stir-fry for 1 minute. Add the remaining ingredients and stir-fry for 2 to 3 more minutes.

3. Serve over warm rice or noodles.

Duck & Rice Side Dish

This classic fried rice recipe is a great way to introduce duck to people who might be on the fence about eating wildfowl meat. You really can't go wrong with a hearty fried rice! The acorn squash should be cut into ½-inch cubes, and the duck breast pieces should be sliced ½ to 1 inch thick.

Ingredients

» 3 tablespoons butter
» 1 tablespoon olive oil
» ¾ cup diced onion
» ¾ cup chopped carrot
» ¾ cup chopped celery
» ½ teaspoon salt
» 1¼ cups chopped acorn squash

» 4 garlic cloves, minced
» 2 cups sliced duck breast
» 1½ cups rice
» ¾ cup chicken broth
» 4 eggs
» Hot sauce, to taste (optional)

Makes: 4 to 6 servings
Prep Time: 15 minutes
Cook Time: 12 to 15 minutes

Preparation

1. Heat the butter and olive oil in a large skillet over medium-high heat. Add the onion, carrot, and celery and sauté until the onions are translucent, about 4 to 5 minutes. Add the salt and acorn squash and cook for 3 more minutes. Add the garlic.

2. Add the duck and cook until lightly browned. Add the rice and chicken broth and stir to combine.

3. Crack the eggs over skillet, keeping the yolks intact, if possible. Cover the skillet with a lid or foil to cook the eggs to your desired temperature. For runny eggs, they are done when the top just turns creamy white. Add a dash or two of hot sauce, if using.

You really can't go wrong with a hearty fried rice!

Broiled Breast of Wild Goose

Any goose hunter knows that all geese are not created equally when it comes to how they translate into the main course of a meal. From the oft-maligned snow goose to a tough old Canada goose, to the really choice specklebelly (greater white-fronted goose), they all behave differently when cooked. This recipe works best with "specks," younger snow geese, and Canada geese. Plate with rice and vegetables for a complete meal.

Makes: 2 to 4 servings

Prep Time:
15 minutes, plus
8 hours marinating

Cook Time:
20 to 25 minutes

Ingredients
» 2 whole wild goose breast fillets
» Salt and pepper, to taste

Marinade
» 1 tablespoon minced onion
» ¼ cup finely shredded carrots
» 2 bay leaves
» ½ teaspoon dried marjoram
» 1 teaspoon dried sage
» 1 teaspoon salt
» ½ teaspoon pepper
» 2 cups white wine

Preparation

1. Season the goose breasts with salt and pepper and place them in a 9 x 13–inch glass baking dish.

2. **Prepare the Marinade.** In a medium bowl, combine the onion, carrots, bay leaves, marjoram, sage, salt, pepper, and white wine and mix well. Pour the Marinade over the goose breasts, turning the breasts to coat both sides. Place the baking dish in the refrigerator for 8 hours to marinate. Turn the breasts over every 2 hours.

3. Preheat the oven broiler. Remove the baking dish from the refrigerator and transfer the goose breasts to a metal rack placed over a baking sheet. Discard the Marinade. Broil the goose uncovered for 11 minutes. Turn the breasts over and broil for an additional 11 minutes or until the meat is cooked to your desired internal temperature. For medium-rare, it should be 130°F to 135°F at the center.

Plate your goose with rice and vegetables for a satisfying meal.

Barbecued Wild Duck

Cooking the duck in parts tends to be easier than cooking the duck whole, but if you're up for the challenge, the result will be the ultimate picture-perfect dish. If you want to cook a whole duck, remove the legs after the breast portions are done and cook them with low, moist heat until the meat pulls away from the bone easily.

Makes: 4 servings

Prep Time: 15 minutes,
plus 12 hours soaking and marinating

Cook Time: 1 hour to
1 hour and 20 minutes

Ingredients

» 2 whole ducks, plucked and cleaned
» 1 tablespoon baking soda

Marinade

» 1 clove garlic
» ½ cup lemon juice
» 1½ cups vegetable oil
» ½ teaspoon dried thyme
» ½ teaspoon celery seed

Barbecue Sauce

» 1½ cups tomato juice
» ¼ cup vinegar
» ½ cup vegetable oil
» 1 tablespoon minced onion
» ½ teaspoon salt
» 1 teaspoon Worcestershire sauce
» 1 tablespoon mustard
» ⅛ teaspoon cayenne pepper
» ½ teaspoon chili powder
» ¼ teaspoon paprika
» ½ teaspoon sugar
» Hot pepper sauce, to taste

Preparation

1. Soak each plucked and cleaned duck in a solution of 1 quart water and 1 tablespoon baking soda for 2 to 3 hours. Rinse the ducks thoroughly and drain. Pat the ducks dry with paper towels.

2. **Prepare the Marinade.** Mince the garlic. In a medium bowl, combine the lemon juice, vegetable oil, thyme, celery seed, and half of the minced garlic. Place the dry ducks in a 9 x 13–inch baking dish and pour the marinade mixture over the ducks. Place the baking dish in the refrigerator for 10 to 12 hours to marinate.

3. Preheat the oven to 350°F. Remove the baking dish from the refrigerator and transfer the ducks to a roasting pan. Discard the Marinade. Roast the ducks uncovered for 15 minutes.

4. **Prepare the Barbecue Sauce.** In a large saucepan over medium heat, combine the tomato juice, vinegar, and vegetable oil. Mix in the onion, salt, Worcestershire sauce, mustard, cayenne pepper, chili powder, paprika, and sugar. Add a few drops of hot pepper sauce. Mix well and bring the mixture to a boil. Reduce the heat and simmer the sauce for 10 minutes.

5. Remove the roasting pan from the oven. Pour half of the Barbecue Sauce over and around the ducks. Cover the roasting pan and return it to the oven to cook for 20 minutes.

6. To serve, place the roasted ducks on a platter. Drizzle the remaining hot Barbecue Sauce over the ducks or serve the sauce on the side.

Cooking the duck in parts tends to be easier than cooking the duck whole, but if you're up for the challenge, it'll be picture-perfect.

Sauces, Vinaigrettes, Marinades & Salsas

Your meat or fish is cooked perfectly, and you want a sauce that complements and enhances its flavor. The grilled venison is the star, the main dish, your show-stopping entrée, but it's almost always true that a drizzle of balsamic or a spoonful of a rich, buttery sauce makes it even tastier. Some cooks prefer to add the sauce to the plate and then set the cooked meat or fish on the sauce. Others simply lay a ribbon of sauce over the meat. Either is good but try not to "bury" your dish with sauce. Less is sometimes more.

The recipes should be considered basic outlines. When you are cooking sauces, marinades, and vinaigrettes, feel free to adjust them to suit your palate. If a sauce or dressing is too sweet, add something acidic like lemon or vinegar to balance the sweetness. Too sour? Add something sweet like a fruit, sugar, or a juice concentrate. Once you get the hang of making sauces, you will only return to the store for emergencies.

There was a time when the word "salsa" was only associated with the tomatoey concoction that always comes with tortilla chips. But today's cooks have learned that the opportunities for salsa are almost limitless. Choosing a salsa should depend on seasonal fruits and vegetables. Just because you can buy a peach in January, doesn't mean you should. The peach likely came from far away, was shipped green and hardly compares to a juicy, ripe July peach. For the best salsas, use ingredients that are at their peak of ripeness.

Tomato and Cucumber Salsa (see page 151) is a classic, light addition to many meals.

Sauces, Vinaigrettes, Marinades & Salsas **139**

The White Wine Butter Sauce is exceptional on quail and other light-fleshed animals.

Red & White Wine Butter Sauces

Conventional culinary wisdom says, "Red wine with meat and white wine with fish" but both of these classic wine sauces pair well with any wild fish preparation. The most common mistake made by home cooks when making a wine reduction sauce is to not reduce the liquid enough before whisking in the chilled butter. For the shallot, you can substitute the white part of a green onion.

Makes: 1½ cups

Ingredients

» 1 cup dry red or white wine
» ½ cup red or white wine vinegar
» 1 tablespoon finely chopped shallot
» 2 cups unsalted butter, cold, cut into small chunks
» Kosher salt, to tasteed

Preparation

1. In a medium saucepan over medium heat, add the wine, vinegar, and shallots. Bring the mixture to a boil, then reduce the heat to low and simmer, uncovered, until the liquid is reduced to about 2 tablespoons.

2. While keeping the pan on low heat, whisk in the chilled butter, a few pieces at a time, but make sure that the butter does not get too hot, or it will break. Keep whisking until only a few pieces of butter are left. Remove the pan from heat, whisk until the remaining butter is emulsified, and season to taste with kosher salt.

No-Fail Hollandaise Sauce

Making a proper hollandaise sauce from scratch seems like a big deal, but this method practically guarantees that yours will be perfect. Once you have made it a time or two, you may want to add other ingredients like orange zest, fresh basil, or tarragon. When adding the butter to the blender, first heat the butter in a microwave or pan until it is bubbling hot, but not broken. At first, add just a few drops, then add it in a thin stream into the egg mixture. The hot butter will "set" the egg yolks to make a creamy sauce. If yours breaks, you added the hot butter too fast. Keep the sauce at room temperature until ready to serve.

Makes: 1 cup

Ingredients

» 3 egg yolks
» ½ teaspoon Dijon mustard
» 1 tablespoon freshly squeezed lemon juice
» 1 cup butter, melted and hot

Preparation

1. Place the egg yolks, Dijon mustard, and lemon juice in a blender or food processor and process until well blended.

2. While the motor is running, add the hot butter, a few drops at a time at first then increasing to a slow, steady stream, until all the butter is incorporated and the sauce is smooth.

Hollandaise is good with any fish meal.

Bourbon-Butter Sauce

Bourbon-Butter Sauce pairs well with any antlered game or waterfowl preparation. When adding flammable liquids like bourbon to a hot pan, make certain that the pan is far from any open flame, i.e., take it some distance away from your active stovetop. Keep your face away from the pan, as the hot pan can possibly ignite the alcohol. This sauce can also be made in the same pan that the meat was cooked in. First, deglaze the pan (away from the heat!) with a splash of bourbon and incorporate the flavor of the cooked meat into the sauce.

Makes: ½ cup

Ingredients
» ¼ cup butter, chilled and divided
» ¼ cup minced onion
» 2 garlic cloves, minced
» 2 teaspoons minced fresh rosemary leaves
» 3 tablespoons bourbon
» 2 teaspoons Dijon mustard
» 2 teaspoons Worcestershire sauce

Preparation
1. Heat 2 tablespoons of the butter in a medium saucepan over medium heat. Add the onion, garlic, and rosemary and cook until the onions are translucent, about 3 to 4 minutes. Stir in the Dijon mustard and Worcestershire sauce. Remove the pan from heat and away from any flame. Stir in the bourbon.

2. Return the pan to heat and simmer for 4 to 5 minutes. Remove the pan from heat and whisk in the remaining 2 tablespoons of chilled butter.

Rustic Tomato & Black Pepper Sauce

This raw, not cooked, sauce is best made with real vine-ripened summer tomatoes—the most flavorful, freshest tomatoes you can get. Using a pepper mill to grind the black pepper right into the sauce gives it that real "rustic" presentation. Perfect for any grilled meats.

Makes: 2 cups

Ingredients
» 4 medium tomatoes, quartered and tossed lightly to dislodge seeds
» 1 cup diced onion
» 3 garlic cloves, minced
» 1 tablespoon cracked peppercorns
» 1 tablespoon dried oregano leaves
» 1 teaspoon sugar

Preparation
1. Combine all the ingredients in a bowl and mix well.

Chimichurri Sauce

A gift to game cooks from our friends in Argentina and Uruguay, this thick green sauce has a very fresh and vibrant edge that enhances wild meat and fish. No need to bury the fish or game with chimichurri; a spoonful or two over the top with additional sauce on the side works best.

Ingredients

» 1 cup packed fresh Italian parsley
» ⅓ cup red wine vinegar
» 2 tablespoons minced fresh oregano leaves
» 5 garlic cloves, minced
» ¾ teaspoon red pepper flakes
» ½ teaspoon salt
» ½ cup extra virgin olive oil

Makes: 1 cup

Preparation

1. Place all the ingredients, except the olive oil, in a food processor, and pulse to blend. In between pulses, scrape the sides of the processor bowl down with a rubber spatula. Transfer the mixture to a medium bowl and whisk in the olive oil.

This sauce packs a punch—a little goes a long way.

Raspberry Vinaigrette & Sauce

If you're short on time and looking for an easy and super-delicious marinade and sauce, this one fits the bill. Soak venison steaks for an hour or so in this marinade before slapping them on a white-hot grill: the sugary raspberry preserves will give the grilled meat crispy, caramelized edges. For extra flavor, baste your meat with the vinaigrette while grilling, and drizzle a little extra over just before serving. Try it on any game and on any oily fish like salmon. It's also great as a salad dressing.

Ingredients
» 2 garlic cloves, minced
» ½ cup raspberry preserves
» ⅓ cup chopped green onions
» ¼ cup balsamic vinegar
» 1 tablespoon Dijon mustard
» 1 cup olive oil
» Salt and pepper, to taste

Makes: 1½ cups

Preparation
1. In a large bowl, whisk together all the ingredients except for the olive oil, salt, and pepper.

2. While whisking, add the olive oil in a thin stream until emulsified. Season to taste with salt and pepper.

Spicy Red Currant & Mustard Sauce

Four ingredients and no cooking are all it takes to prepare this delicious-yet-complex sauce that pairs well with anything wrapped in bacon, upland game like pheasant, wild turkey, or quail, and salmon. If you have access to fresh red currants and want to go the extra mile, you can make your own red currant jelly.

Ingredients
» ⅔ cup red currant jelly
» ⅓ cup Dijon mustard
» 1 teaspoon freshly squeezed lemon juice
» 1 teaspoon red pepper flakes

Makes: 1 cup

Preparation
1. Combine all the ingredients in a bowl and mix well.

Orange-Ginger Sauce

This sauce is a little sweet, a little sour, and just salty enough to give your grilled game meats a lift. The orange juice concentrate adds a sweet and citrusy flavor that blends incredibly well with the zing of pickled ginger, the umami flavor of soy, and rice vinegar's sour.

Ingredients

» ⅔ cup orange juice concentrate, plus more as needed
» ⅓ cup soy sauce
» ¼ cup rice vinegar, plus more as needed
» 2 tablespoons minced pickled ginger

Makes: 1¼ cups

Preparation

1. Combine all the ingredients in a bowl.

2. Adjust the sauce's flavor to suit your palate: too sour? Add more orange juice concentrate. Too sweet? Add more rice vinegar.

Apricot-Horseradish Sauce

This three-ingredient recipe might surprise you with its unexpected balance of sweet, hot, and sour flavors. Great as a dipping sauce or spooned over any wild game preparation. Try brushing it onto grilling meats just a few minutes before removing the meat from the flame. Use prepared horseradish, not creamed, the higher the quality the better.

Ingredients

» ½ cup horseradish
» ½ cup apricot preserves
» 1 tablespoon freshly squeezed lemon juice

Makes: 1 cup

Preparation

1. Combine all the ingredients in a bowl and mix well.

Champagne Cream Sauce

This special-occasion sauce that combines sparkling white wine with heavy cream makes a perfectly cooked piece of fish taste that much better. If champagne (or prosecco) isn't available, try it with a decent dry white wine. You can substitute the white part of two green onions for the shallot if desired.

Ingredients

» 2 cups dry champagne
» ¼ cup lemon juice
» 1 shallot, minced
» ½ cup heavy cream
» 3 tablespoons butter, chilled
» Salt and white pepper, to taste

Makes: 1 cup

Preparation

1. In a large skillet over medium heat, combine the champagne, lemon juice, and shallot. Bring the mixture to a boil then lower the heat and simmer for 10 to 12 minutes, until the liquid is reduced to about ⅓ cup.

2. Whisk in the chilled butter until emulsified, then quickly remove the skillet from heat. Season to taste with salt and white pepper.

Herb Vinaigrette & Marinade

Herb Vinaigrette & Marinade gives you a real workhorse marinade, sauce, or dressing to add flavor to your fish, game, or salad. Because of the acidity from the vinegar and lemon juice, limit the marinating time to two or three hours, especially with fish: too long in the marinade will "cook" fish much like ceviche.

Ingredients

» 2 garlic cloves, minced
» ½ cup white wine vinegar
» ½ cup olive oil
» ⅓ cup chopped fresh herbs
» 1 tablespoon freshly squeezed lemon juice
» 1 teaspoon Dijon mustard
» ½ teaspoon sugar

Makes: 1⅓ cups

Preparation

1. Combine all the ingredients in a jar with a tight-fitting lid and shake vigorously.

Artichoke & Basil Sauce

This is a simple sauce for fish that can be prepared in the blender in just a few minutes. You can heat it slowly in a saucepan, but if you do, don't bring it to a boil. Spoon this zesty, rich sauce over just-cooked fish and you're good to go. You can buy the artichoke hearts at the store, typically in the jar.

Ingredients

- » 1 cup fresh basil leaves
- » ⅔ cup marinated artichoke hearts
- » Juice of 1 lemon
- » 2 garlic cloves, minced
- » 3 tablespoons grated Parmesan cheese
- » 2 tablespoons almonds, lightly toasted in a 325°F oven
- » ¼ cup olive oil
- » Salt and pepper, to taste

Makes: 1 cup

Preparation

1. Combine all the ingredients, except the olive oil, salt, and pepper, in a blender or food processor and pulse to process until the mixture is almost pureed but still a little chunky.

2. While the motor is running, add the olive oil in a thin stream until emulsified. Season with salt and pepper to taste.

Horseradish Cream Sauce

If you enjoy a horseradish sauce on prime rib—that steak house staple—you will absolutely love it on deer, elk, or waterfowl. Always use prepared horseradish, not creamed. The higher the quality of the horseradish you use, the more unforgettable your dish will be.

Ingredients

- » 1 tablespoon olive oil
- » 2 green onions, diced
- » 1 garlic clove, minced
- » 1 teaspoon minced fresh rosemary leaves
- » ¼ cup dry white wine
- » ½ teaspoon Worcestershire sauce
- » 2 to 3 tablespoons horseradish
- » ¾ cup heavy whipping cream

Makes: 1 cup

Preparation

1. Heat the olive oil in a small saucepan over medium heat. Add the green onions, garlic, and rosemary and cook for 1 minute.

2. Add the white wine and Worcestershire sauce and continue to cook until the liquid is reduced by one-half. Stir in the horseradish and cream and bring to just below boiling while stirring. Allow the sauce to cool.

Sauces, Vinaigrettes, Marinades & Salsas **147**

Basic Duck Marinade

Despite the name, this marinade is not just for ducks; it also adds flavor to antlered game and feral hog meat. Add a little extra time in the marinade for darker-fleshed ducks like divers and sea ducks. To best use this marinade, pour it over your duck meat in a large dish and keep the dish in the refrigerator for 6 to 24 hours, turning the meat occasionally. Before cooking, discard the marinade and pat the meat dry with paper towels.

Makes: 1 quart

Ingredients

- » 1 medium onion, diced
- » 6 garlic cloves, minced
- » 2 cups dry red wine
- » ½ cup soy sauce
- » ¼ cup balsamic or red wine vinegar
- » ¼ cup vegetable oil
- » 1 teaspoon cracked peppercorns

Preparation

1. Combine all the ingredients in a container with a tight-fitting lid and shake well.

Chili Lemon-Lime Marinade

The lime really perks up the flavors of this spicy marinade that's great on salmon, tuna, and just about any wild game. You don't need to smother the fish or meat with this marinade—a little goes a long way! If you prefer more spice, use more jalapeños, or keep some of the seeds in.

Makes: 2 cups

Ingredients

- » 5 garlic cloves, minced
- » 1 jalapeño, seeded and minced
- » 2 teaspoons kosher salt
- » 1 teaspoon chili powder
- » ½ cup sugar
- » 1 teaspoon freshly ground black pepper
- » ¾ cup freshly squeezed lime juice
- » ½ cup freshly squeezed lemon juice
- » ¼ cup minced red onion
- » 5 to 6 sprigs fresh cilantro, chopped
- » ¼ cup olive oil

Preparation

1. Combine the garlic, jalapeño, salt, chili powder, sugar, and pepper in a bowl or mortar and pestle and mash them together with the back side of a large spoon or pestle.
2. Add the lime juice, lemon juice, red onion, and cilantro and mix well. While stirring, drizzle the olive oil into the mixture.

Balsamic Blackberry Glaze

Reducing balsamic vinegar intensifies its oaky flavors and the blackberries help bring out its layered sweetness. Keep this rich glaze on hand year-round for a quick finishing touch for salmon and grilled meats. The blackberries can be frozen or fresh.

Ingredients

» 3 cups balsamic vinegar, plus 1 teaspoon
» 1 cup blackberries
» ½ teaspoon cornstarch

Makes: 1 cup

Preparation

1. Add 3 cups of the vinegar and the berries to a medium saucepan and bring the mixture to a boil. Reduce the heat and simmer until the liquid has been reduced to about 1½ cups.

2. In a cup, whisk the cornstarch with 1 teaspoon of balsamic vinegar. Strain the berries out through a strainer and return the liquid to the pan, making sure all the berry seeds have been removed.

3. Bring the liquid to a boil and stir in the cornstarch mixture, a little at a time, until the sauce thickens. Allow the glaze to cool and transfer it to a squeeze bottle.

Caper-Dill Vinaigrette & Marinade

Something about dill and salmon together is just delicious. The key is to cook or, better yet, grill your salmon first and then drizzle this vinaigrette over the fish and let sit for the last five minutes. It's a pairing that always works.

Ingredients

» 4 tablespoons white wine vinegar
» 1 garlic clove, minced
» ½ tablespoon Dijon mustard
» ¼ teaspoon sugar
» ¾ cup olive oil
» 1 tablespoon chopped fresh dill
» 1 tablespoon capers, drained
» ½ teaspoon lemon zest
» Salt and pepper, to taste

Makes: 1 cup

Preparation

1. In a medium bowl, whisk together the vinegar, garlic, Dijon mustard, and sugar. While whisking vigorously, drizzle in the olive oil until emulsified.

2. Stir in the remaining ingredients and season with salt and pepper.

Onion, Jalapeño & Cranberry Relish

Serve this at holiday gatherings instead of your usual cranberry relish—most people will be surprised at how well jalapeño and cranberries go together. This can be made several days in advance and stored in the refrigerator. Be sure to allow it to rest at room temperature for an hour before serving and you'll make a memorable impression on your fellow guests' palates.

Makes: 1½ cups

Ingredients

- » 3 tablespoons olive oil
- » 4 cups diced onion
- » 2 to 3 jalapeños, seeded and minced
- » ½ teaspoon salt
- » Pinch black pepper
- » 1 cup red wine vinegar
- » ½ cup dried cranberries
- » ⅓ cup light brown sugar
- » ¼ cup balsamic vinegar

Preparation

1. Heat the olive oil in a large skillet over high heat. Add the onions, jalapeño, salt, and pepper and cook until the onions are light brown, stirring occasionally.

2. Stir in the remaining ingredients and simmer, uncovered, until the liquid has evaporated, about 20 to 25 minutes. Serve warm.

Chipotle-Citrus Marinade

This marinade is best used with firm, oily to semi-oily fish—salmon, yellowtail, dorado, and any species of tuna. Be sure to limit the marinating time to just an hour or two to avoid oversoaking the fish. This salsa is great for when you want to give your fish preparation that Tex-Mex flavor.

Ingredients

- » 2 chipotle chiles from the can, with adobo sauce
- » 4 garlic cloves
- » ¾ cup orange juice
- » ¼ cup olive oil
- » ¼ cup roughly chopped onion
- » 1 tablespoon freshly squeezed lime juice
- » 1 tablespoon freshly squeezed lemon juice
- » 1 tablespoon apple cider vinegar
- » 2 teaspoons sugar
- » 1 teaspoon dried oregano leaves
- » ⅛ teaspoon black pepper
- » ⅛ teaspoon salt

Makes: 1½ cups

Preparation

1. In a food processor or blender, add all the ingredients except the olive oil and process until pureed.

2. While the motor is running, add the olive oil in a thin stream until emulsified.

Tomato & Cucumber Salsa

When summer is reaching its peak and the tomato plants are high and the cucumber vines heavy with produce, head out to the garden with your pruners and collect the goods for this savory, tangy salsa that's full of veggie freshness. Pairs well with any fish and any upland game bird preparation. Don't forget the basket of tortilla chips.

Ingredients

- 1 cup halved red grape tomatoes
- ½ cup peeled, seeded, and diced cucumbers
- 3 tablespoons slivered almonds, lightly toasted
- 2 tablespoons chopped black olives
- 2 tablespoons minced red onion
- 2 tablespoons minced fresh cilantro leaves
- 1 tablespoon freshly squeezed lime juice
- 1 tablespoon olive oil
- Dash Tabasco sauce
- Pinch ground cumin
- Salt and pepper, to taste

Makes: 2 cups

Preparation

1. Combine all the ingredients in a bowl and toss gently. Allow the salsa to rest at room temperature for 15 minutes before serving.

Plum Salsa

Plum salsa is not only an exciting and rare salsa, it also pairs well with any fish preparation but also give it a shot with upland game like quail, wild turkey, or rabbit. Be sure to give it its 30-minute rest at room temperature, because that's when the flavors really combine to perfection.

Ingredients

- 3 medium ripe plums, seeds removed and chopped
- 1 jalapeño, seeded and minced
- ¼ cup finely diced red onion
- ¼ cup finely diced red bell pepper
- 2 tablespoons minced cilantro leaves
- 2 tablespoons rice vinegar
- 1 teaspoon lime juice
- ½ teaspoon peeled and minced fresh ginger
- ¼ teaspoon sesame oil
- Dash Asian hot chili sauce

Makes: 1 cup

Preparation

1. Combine all the ingredients in a bowl and toss lightly to combine. Let the salsa rest at room temperature for 30 minutes before serving.

This salsa pairs well—very well—with fish tacos.

Mango Pico de Gallo

In Spanish, *pico de gallo* means "rooster's beak" because the dish was originally eaten with the thumb and forefinger, resembling a rooster pecking. Some people really load up on the cilantro and if that's what's in your garden, there's no better way to use it. Chop the mango into ¼-inch cubes.

Makes: 2 cups

Ingredients

» 1 jalapeño, seeded and minced
» 1½ cups peeled, seeded, and diced mango
» 3 tablespoons red bell pepper, finely chopped
» 2 tablespoons minced cilantro leaves
» 2 tablespoons seasoned rice vinegar
» Juice of 1 lime
» Pinch salt
» Pinch freshly ground black pepper

Preparation

1. Combine all the ingredients in a bowl and mix well. Refrigerate for 1 hour before serving.

Mandarin Orange & Avocado Salsa

This salsa pairs well with any fish—grilled, broiled, pan-seared, or fried. If you have prepared your fish on the spicy side, this salsa will help balance the fire with its citrus notes and cool, clean avocado texture. For a surf-friendly twist on this recipe, mix in 1 cup of cooked bay shrimp.

Makes: 2 cups

Ingredients

» 1 cup mandarin segments, most of the white part removed
» 1 large avocado
» 2 garlic cloves, minced
» 1 jalapeño, seeded and minced
» ¼ cup finely minced red onion
» ¼ cup diced red bell pepper
» 2 tablespoons olive oil
» 1 tablespoon minced cilantro leaves
» 1 tablespoon freshly squeezed lime juice
» Pinch ground cumin
» Pinch chili powder
» Salt, to taste

Preparation

1. Combine all the ingredients in a glass, ceramic, or plastic bowl and toss gently to mix. Allow the salsa to rest at room temperature for 30 minutes before serving.

Cherry Tomato & Green Olive Salsa

There's just no comparing the flavor and freshness of ripe, homegrown tomatoes with their grocery store counterparts. For this dish to be its best, head out to your backyard garden's tomato vines or to your nearest farmers market.

Makes: 1½ cups

Ingredients

» 1 cup halved cherry tomatoes
» ¼ cup sliced pitted green olives
» 2 green onions, minced
» 2 tablespoons minced fresh cilantro leaves
» 1 tablespoon minced fresh oregano leaves
» 1 tablespoon freshly squeezed lemon juice
» 1 tablespoon balsamic vinegar
» 1 teaspoon chili powder
» 1 teaspoon honey
» Salt and pepper, to taste

Preparation

1. Combine all the ingredients, except the salt and pepper, in a bowl and mix well. Season to taste with salt and pepper.

This mango salsa is the perfect sweet and spicy blend of light, summery flavors and heat.

Mango Salsa

Mango freshens up any salsa with a sweet, fruity flavor, but be encouraged to experiment with fruits like papaya and watermelon, too. And if you're game for a spicier kick, try using a Thai chili, or another pepper that gives you as much heat as you can handle, in place of the jalapeño.

Makes: 1 cup

Ingredients

- » 1 jalapeño
- » 1 mango, diced
- » 1 small cucumber, peeled, seeded, and diced
- » 1 avocado
- » Juice of 2 limes
- » ½ medium red onion, chopped
- » Cilantro leaves, chopped, to taste
- » ¼ cup light brown sugar
- » 1 teaspoon ground cumin

Preparation

1. Roast the chile pepper over an open flame such as a stovetop, using a metal skewer to hold the pepper over the heat, until it is completely charred on the outside.

2. Peel off the charred skin and dice the pepper. Place the diced pepper in a small bowl and mix in the remaining ingredients. Allow the salsa to rest at room temperature for 10 minutes before serving.

Grilled Corn & Black Bean Salsa

This recipe is perfect for that time of year when the tomatoes are ripe on the vine, the sweet corn is stacked high at farmers markets, and the urge to grill is easy to please: summertime.

Ingredients

- » 3 ears sweet corn, husks and silk removed
- » 1 small red bell pepper, halved and seeded
- » 1 small green bell pepper, halved and seeded
- » 1 medium red onion, sliced into ¼-inch-thick slices
- » 3 tablespoons olive oil
- » 1 cup black beans, drained, rinsed, and cooked
- » 1 cup fresh tomato, seeded and diced
- » 3 tablespoons chopped cilantro leaves
- » 2 garlic cloves, minced
- » 2 tablespoons freshly squeezed lime juice
- » 1 to 2 dashes Tabasco sauce
- » Salt and pepper, to taste

Makes: 3 to 4 cups

Preparation

1. Preheat a grill to high heat. Rub the corn, peppers, and onion with 2 tablespoons of the olive oil and place them on the white-hot grill.

2. Grill until the corn is lightly browned and the peppers are charred. Remove the charred skins from the peppers (leaving some of the charred skin is fine) and remove the corn kernels from the cobs.

3. Combine the corn, peppers, and onion with the remaining ingredients and let the salsa rest at room temperature for 1 hour before serving.

Pair this treat with grilled fish, tortilla chips, and a long pleasant evening in the garden or on the back patio.

Index

Unless otherwise noted, recipe photography provided by Scott Leysath.
The following images are from Shutterstock.com: animal graphics throughout: Duda Vasilii, PhotoHouse, Danler, Abel Hanz, Jollanda, Hennadii H, Myurenn, and redrangerstudio; 3 left, 47: Karl Allgaeuer; 3 center: DronG; 3 right: Douglas Freer; 4–5, 58: Netrun78; 5, 79: Maren Winter; 5, 113: Natasha Breen; 5, 80, 155: Joshua Resnick; 6–7: ABO PHOTOGRAPHY; 10: hlphoto; 13: Slawomir Fajer; 15: Slavica Stajic; 17: stockcreations; 19: IgorPloskin; 21: Timolina; 28: Go My Media; 29: hlphoto; 33: P Maxwell Photography; 37: Jack Dagley Photography; 38, 152: Brent Hofacker; 42: Karin Hildebrand Lau; 43: Kuxcen; 45, 102: New Africa; 46: Jacek Chabraszewski; 53: lv-olga; 56: YARUNIV Studio; 57, 98: Alexander Prokopenko; 61: Alpha_7D; 63: Lunov Mykola; 66: Piotr Wawrzyniuk; 67: Jennifer White Maxwell; 70, 154: AS Foodstudio; 71: Kiian Oksana; 73: Wirestock Creators; 74: Nataly Studio; 81: Ms. Trouble Maker; 84, 95: HandmadePictures; 89: Peredniankina; 90: Michelle Lee Photography; 91: DUSAN ZIDAR; 92: Bigc Studio; 94: Oliver Hoffman; 97: Mironov Vladimir; 99: Ksenia Raykova; 101: mipstudio; 103: Elzbieta Sekowska; 104: Fabian Montano Hernandez; 105: Sokor Space; 107: Angelika Heine; 109: gkrphoto; 111: Tetiana Chernykova; 114: Africa Studio; 115: OlgaBombologna; 116: Eugene PLISHKIN; 117: zorinjonny; 120: JJ-stockstudio; 126: Cacio Murilo; 127: Peter Kim; 129: freeskyline; 131: Joe Gough; 133: Ratov Maxim; 139: Tereza Tsyaulouskaya; 140: Serghhei Starus; 141: Marcel Fulsche; 143: Axel Mel

About the Editor

Chef Scott Leysath is the author of three fish and game cookbooks. He is a columnist for several publications on hunting, fishing, and outdoor life. Leysath is also a television producer and host, most notably with *The Sporting Chef* and *Dead Meat* series on Outdoor Channel. He is passionate about making anything with fins, fur, and feathers come deliciously alive.